The Generic Qualitative Approach to a Dissertation in the Social Sciences

The Generic Qualitative Approach to a Dissertation in the Social Sciences: A Step by Step Guide is a practical guide for the graduate students and faculties planning and executing a generic qualitative dissertation in the social sciences.

Generic qualitative research is a methodology that seeks to understand human experience by taking a qualitative stance and using qualitative procedures. Based on Sandra Kostere and Kim Kostere's experiences of serving on dissertation committees, this book aims to demystify both the nuances and the procedures of qualitative research, with the aim of empowering students to conduct meaningful dissertation research and present findings that are rigorous, credible, and trustworthy. It examines the fundamental principles and assumptions underlying the generic qualitative method, then covers each stage of the research process including creation of research questions, interviews, and then offers three ways of analyzing the data gathered and presenting the results.

With examples of the generic qualitative method in practice to show students how to conduct their research confidently, and chapters designed to walk the researcher through each step of the dissertation process, this book is specifically tailored for the accessible generic method, and will be useful for graduate students and faculty developing dissertations in Psychology, Education, Nursing, and the Social Sciences.

Sandra Kostere received her Ph.D. from The Union Institute in 1989. She studied qualitative research with Clark Moustakas. She is a co-author of the journal article, "Generic Qualitative Research in Psychology" (2015). She served as a faculty member at Capella University for 20 years. She taught advanced qualitative research, served as a qualitative research consultant, and chaired qualitative dissertations.

Kim Kostere received his Ph.D. from The Union Institute in 1989. He studied qualitative research with Clark Moustakas. He is a co-author of the journal article, "Generic Qualitative Research in Psychology" (2015). He served as a faculty member at Capella University for 20 years. He taught advanced qualitative research and has served as a chair and committee member for qualitative dissertations.

The Generic Qualitative Approach to a Dissertation in the Social Sciences

A Step by Step Guide

Sandra Kostere and Kim Kostere

Routledge
Taylor & Francis Group

LONDON AND NEW YORK

First published 2022
by Routledge
2 Park Square, Milton Park, Abingdon, Oxon OX14 4RN

and by Routledge
605 Third Avenue, New York, NY 10158

Routledge is an imprint of the Taylor & Francis Group, an informa business

© 2022 Sandra Kostere and Kim Kostere

British Library Cataloguing-in-Publication Data
A catalogue record for this book is available from the British Library

Library of Congress Cataloging-in-Publication Data
A catalog record has been requested for this book

ISBN: 978-1-032-05022-5 (hbk)
ISBN: 978-1-032-05024-9 (pbk)
ISBN: 978-1-003-19568-9 (ebk)

DOI: 10.4324/9781003195689

Typeset in Galliard
by codeMantra

To Hannah Shakespeare, Senior Commissioning Editor, for her knowledge, guidance, and valuable support.

To Clark Moustakas our teacher and our friend. We will always remember and cherish our experiences in Nova Scotia.

To educators who created our original desire for conducting qualitative research, Bruce Douglass, Cereta Perry, and Gerald Wehmer.

Appreciation to colleagues who have contributed to the development of the generic qualitative approach as a credible method of research: Bill Percy, Malcolm Gray, Lou Kuvar, and Rosanne Roberts.

Recognition of past theorists who have inspired meaningful ways of thinking which inspired the importance of qualitative research as an essential way for understanding human thoughts, feelings, and behavior; Carl Rogers, Rollo May, Viktor Frankl, Abraham Maslow, Amedeo Giorgi, Kathy Charmaz.

To our dissertation students for the joy of watching their processes during their dissertations. For the experience of observing students flourish through a mixture of awareness, enthusiasm, excitement, and A-Ha experiences.

The Center for Humanistic Studies, an amazing learning experience and the beginning of our qualitative research journey.

As always, Tracey and Paul.

Contents

Beginning the journey

This book is designed to serve as a guide for both students and faculty who are developing dissertations using a generic qualitative approach. Included in this book are instructions for developing a dissertation research question, methods and procedures for collecting and analyzing data, and suggestions for presenting the results of a generic qualitative dissertation. Since the generic qualitative dissertation incorporates *essential* characteristics of the qualitative approach to research, it is our belief that in order to conduct a credible generic qualitative dissertation, the journey includes knowledge and understanding about the underpinnings of qualitative research.

What is generic qualitative research?

The defining of generic qualitative research has been elusive, as thus far the definitions tend to ponder on *what it is not* instead of *what it is*. Caelli et al. (2003) discussed generic qualitative research as "…qualitative studies that have no guiding set of philosophic assumptions in the form of one of the established qualitative methodologies" (p. 1). Merriam

DOI: 10.4324/9781003195689-1

(2009) discussed the struggle of trying to define qualitative studies that do not follow a specific theoretical framework. She used the terms "generic, basic, and interpretive" (p. 22). Percy et al. (2015) indicated that generic qualitative research is used when the topic is not appropriate for any of the traditional qualitative models. Kennedy (2016) implied that in order to start understanding generic qualitative inquiry it is helpful to define what it is not.

In an earlier book by Merriam (1998), she suggested that generic qualitative studies "...simply seek to discover and understand a phenomenon, a process, or the perspectives and worldviews of the people involved" (p. 11). More recently, Patton (2015) described generic qualitative inquiry as a practical approach that involves skillfully using qualitative methods to answer questions about relevant topics in a real-world setting (pp. 154–155).

The discussions on generic qualitative research in the literature support the need for developing a clearer definition, identifiable methods and procedures, and the understanding of the researcher's theoretical position. According to Caelli et al. (2003), descriptions defining and explaining generic qualitative research have been "clear as mud" because "... the literature lacks debate about how to do a generic study well" (Abstract). Cooper and Endacott (2007) stated, "This generic approach is no doubt selected for pragmatic reasons but can be weakened by a lack of rigor and understanding of qualitative research" (p. 816). Caelli et al. (2003), Cooper and Endacott (2007), and Aronson (1994) indicated the need for explicit requirements for conducting generic qualitative research, and clarity about the procedures that assure rigor and trustworthiness in generic qualitative studies.

Throughout the search for a consensus of what generic qualitative research means, we reflected on the interpretations and concerns expressed about the generic qualitative approach, thus far in the literature. Therefore, we used these interpretations and concerns to develop the following working definition as the guideline for this book. *Generic qualitative research is a methodology that seeks to understand human experience by taking a qualitative stance and using qualitative procedures.*

How will I know if generic qualitative research fits for my dissertation research question?

Good question! Selecting the research methodology that will answer your research question is an important step towards a credible and meaningful dissertation. Your research design needs to correspond with answering your research question. In determining whether a generic qualitative design fits for your dissertation there are three basic questions to consider: Does your research question seek an understanding of human experience? Are you using qualitative procedures? Is your research design consistent with a qualitative stance?

Understanding human experience

When seeking to understand human experience, your research question explores how people make sense out of their experiences. Understanding human experience relates to how people construct meaning interrelated to themselves, others, social situations, and world occurrences.

According to Patton (2015), "The first contribution of qualitative inquiry, then, is illuminating meanings and how humans engage in meaning making – in essence, making sense of the world" (p. 6). The generic qualitative research dissertation seeks to illuminate and interpret meanings of the phenomenon under inquiry based on the individual perceptions and experiences described by the participants.

The qualitative stance

The qualitative stance refers to the researcher's thinking and beliefs about what the important goals are for human science research. According to Camic et al. (2003), the heart of the qualitative stance is "the desire to make sense of actual lived experience" (p. 56). Merriam (2009) asserted, "A central characteristic of qualitative research is that individuals construct reality in interaction with their social worlds" (p. 22). Berger and Luckmann's (1966) theory on social constructivism suggests that reality is emergent and is created or constructed by social interaction. Thus, the qualitative stance values understanding how individuals construct meaning from their experiences.

Camic et al. (2003) declared that researchers assuming a qualitative stance have different goals than researchers conducting laboratory experiments. Qualitative research is conducted in a natural setting in order to understand the participants in the context of their real-life experiences. The qualitative researcher asks about human action and meanings during social and cultural interactions. The qualitative stance embraces the first-person narrative and asks questions that encourage descriptive data. Researchers strives for discovery, understanding, and meaning. They search for a wider range and more complex understandings of human experiences.

The qualitative stance requires the researcher to identify and set aside pre-understandings and pre-suppositions for the purpose of staying open to individual differences, the unknown and new potential meanings. According to Dahlberg et al. (2002), "Openness is always constrained by pre-understanding. In all research, quantitative as well as qualitative, we have to deal with our pre-suppositions in order to remain open throughout the whole process of inquiry" (p. 118). The researcher identifies their pre-understandings and pre-suppositions, and takes care not to allow pre-suppositions to influence those interpretations.

The qualitative stance values the philosophical beliefs underpinning qualitative research. Tashakkori and Teddlie (1998) referred to the "axioms of the naturalist paradigm" (p. 19), which include understanding and embracing the following axioms:

- *Ontology* (the nature of reality): Naturalists believe that there are multiple, constructed realities.
- *Epistemology* (the relationship of the knower to the known): Naturalists believe that the knower and the known are inseparable.
- *Axiology* (the role of values in inquiry): Naturalists believe that inquiry is value-bound.
- *Generalizations:* Naturalists believe that time- and context-free generalizations are not possible.
- *Causal linkages:* Naturalists believe that it is impossible to distinguish causes from effects.
- *Inductive logic:* There is an emphasis on arguing from the particular to the general, or an emphasis on "grounded" theory (p. 19).

Qualitative procedures

Qualitative research uses procedures that generate descriptive data (Taylor & Bogdan, 1998). The most commonly used procedure for collecting qualitative data is the qualitative interviews. For a generic qualitative dissertation, semi-structured interviews are recommended; if the study warrants a more in-depth exploration of the topic, the open-ended conversational interview is suggested. Other conceivable forms of data for a generic qualitative dissertation might include journals, diaries, unsent or sent letters, documents, observations, photographs, memos, and field notes (see Chapter 5). In a generic qualitative dissertation, the focus is on words and language, not numbers and measurements. The data collection process seeks out rich descriptions of people's experiences.

There is a strong emphasis on the researcher's commitment to qualitative procedures. Patton (2002) claimed, "In qualitative inquiry, the researcher is the instrument. The credibility of qualitative methods, therefore, hinge to a great extent on the skill, competence, and rigor of the person doing the field-work..." (p. 14). The qualitative procedure for data analysis is based on an inductive reasoning process. The quality of the data analysis depends on the researcher's familiarization with the data, reasoning skills, and their openness to creative and intuitive processes.

The data analysis procedure is conducted in a step-by-step process. The data presentation in your dissertation provides visibility of the specific steps of the data analysis process. The presentation of data includes the researcher's interpretations along with supporting data in the form of direct quotation from the transcribed interviews or other data collected from the participants. The steps and results of the analysis are reflected in a manner that allows the reader to understand and conceptualize how the data were collected, analyzed, and interpreted. The reader of the data analysis section in a generic qualitative dissertation should be able to say, *I understand how the researcher came up with the results and the results make sense. Now I truly understand the experience of ...* The results should be clear to anyone, even if they are not familiar with qualitative research.

What qualities are needed to become a qualitative researcher?

New researchers need to... understand the language of qualitative inquiry, and to know what questions to ask, where to look for information and how to start thinking qualitatively.

(Morse & Richards, 2002, p. xiii)

Becoming a qualitative researcher for many requires a paradigm shift, since most college students were educationally brought up learning the quantitative research philosophy, using variables and measurements, and asking cause and effect-oriented research questions. Stake (2010) stated, "Qualitative research has moved social research away from an emphasis on cause-and-effect explanation and toward personal interpretation" (p. 41). However, the shift towards thinking qualitatively requires exposure to and knowledge of the qualitative paradigm. During our time teaching beginning courses in qualitative research, we became aware that students tended to use quantitative terminology to interpret qualitative research procedures. We determined that comprehending the language of qualitative research was essential for thinking qualitatively, and that the appropriate language was essential for a successful paradigm shift.

Learning the qualitative language involves exposure to credible qualitative research literature. When teaching beginning qualitative research, the textbooks for the course were books by Michael Quinn Patton and John W. Creswell. Both authors offer a clear and thorough introduction to qualitative research. Be aware of authors who use quantitative language when discussing qualitative methods. For example, some research textbooks discuss qualitative studies using vocabulary that is inconsistent with the qualitative stance; some authors include terms such as hypothesis, variables, subjects, and generalizability, which are related to the quantitative stance. That said, qualitative research and quantitative research are *different* paradigms used for *different purposes*. One does not *translate* one to the other because they are like apples and oranges. For example, one cannot translate *causation* from quantitative language to qualitative language, because *causation* does not exist in qualitative research. When translating materials from the quantitative paradigm to a qualitative paradigm, the essence of the qualitative paradigm is lost in the translation.

Becoming a qualitative researcher begins with recognizing and understanding qualitative research language. Some of the common words used in qualitative research studies are experience, discovery, understanding, meaning, exploration, process, involvement, passion, commitment, themes, patterns, sensitivity, intuition, illumination, creativity, lived experience, and first-person narrative. You will be exposed to qualitative language throughout this book. If you find that these words capture your interest, you are on track for becoming a qualitative researcher.

The qualitative researcher often chooses a topic that has personal meaning. Therefore, the qualitative dissertation process becomes one of passion and commitment. However, because of the researcher's personal experiences with the topic, it is necessary to identify personal beliefs about the topic under investigation and set aside pre-understandings. The qualitative researcher strives to come from the position of not knowing and not judging, thus respecting the uniqueness of the experience for each participant.

The qualitative researcher acknowledges qualitative research as evidence of scientific investigation. They value data obtained through first-person narratives and believe that data describe human experience as "imperative in understanding human behavior" (Moustakas, 1994, p. 21).

In conclusion of the criteria for becoming a qualitative researcher, a childhood book comes to mind. This quote from *The Little Prince* offers a metaphor that can be used as an example of the differences between quantitative and qualitative thinking.

> If I have told you these details about the Asteroid B-612 and if I've given you its number, it is on account of grown-ups and their ways. Grown-ups love numbers. When you tell them about a new friend, they never ask you any questions about what really matters. They never say to you, "What does his voice sound like? What game does he like

best? Does he collect butterflies?" They ask: "How old is he? How many brothers does he have? How much does he weigh? How much money does his father make?" Only then do they think they know him.

(de Saint-Exupery, 1943, p. 10)

What to expect in this book?

The background for this book began with a handout that was developed containing a brief overview of generic qualitative research (Generic Qualitative Research in Psychology, Capella University, Percy et al., 2008). The journal article "Generic Qualitative Research in Psychology" (Percy et al., 2015) was published in *The Qualitative Report*, Nova Southeastern University. The article provided more detail than the unpublished handout about applying this research model and contained methods to promote academic rigor. As of the end of February 2021, there have been **15,742** copies of the article downloaded, thereby indicating an interest in development and clarification of the generic qualitative approach.

Because of the change in focus from research in general to specifically dissertations, and based on our experiences of mentoring dissertation students, we have made necessary changes from the information presented in the article "Generic Qualitative Research in Psychology" (Percy et al., 2015) to address the needs required for a dissertation. We have added more options regarding topics and added specific methodological procedures for conducting a generic qualitative dissertation with respect for the time limits inherent in the dissertation process.

In this chapter we have identified and discussed the concerns stated in the literature on generic qualitative research about the lack of clarity in the *methods,* rigor, and *trustworthiness.* This book intends to address the *why* and *how* of the generic approach by clearly identifying a step-by-step explanation of methods and procedures, and providing guidelines for demonstrating rigor and trustworthiness. Although generic qualitative research can be used for a variety of reasons, this book will only focus on the details and the practicality of using the generic qualitative approach to conduct a dissertation in the social sciences.

In Chapter 2, you will begin your dissertation journey. The journey begins with learning how to develop a qualitative research question. This will include discussing questions that are suitable for a generic qualitative dissertation, the type of topics that work best for qualitative studies, and topics and questions to avoid.

CHAPTER 2

The research question

The generic qualitative approach to dissertation research allows for a diversity of topics. However, approval of dissertation topics is conditional to the educational institution. Each university has its own specifications for topics and research questions inside each department within the social sciences. It is important for students to investigate their university guidelines prior to developing the research topic.

Most books and articles are written about qualitative research in general and do not specifically focus on a dissertation. Thus, students often find that the initial scope of their study is unrealistic for a dissertation. The following guidelines need to be considered when developing the qualitative research plan. A qualitative dissertation needs to have a balance of rigor *within a doable time frame* for a doctoral level dissertation. When the doctoral student selects a topic, it is usually a topic of special interest. This may lead to trying to accomplish more than is possible for a dissertation. A qualitative design has many possibilities, and it is necessary for the doctoral student to remain aware of time restraints. Further research can be accomplished after completing the doctoral degree.

DOI: 10.4324/9781003195689-2

The generic qualitative dissertation is led by one research question. "The essence of the question is the opening up and keeping open, of possibility" (Gadamer, 1975, p. 226). This question must be open-ended and focused on seeking understanding and discovery. The question should name the phenomenon. In a generic qualitative dissertation, only one phenomenon is under inquiry. Finally, the student must be able to answer the research question by using qualitative methods and procedures.

Developing an achievable dissertation research question is essential for a successful dissertation. We cannot over emphasize the centrality of a clear, well-stated research question. In essence, the research question for qualitative research guides the overall research design. There must be an agreement, continuity, and a logical connection between the research question and the rest of the qualitative research design. The ingredients for developing a generic qualitative research question for a dissertation begins with relevance, clarity, and consistency with qualitative methods.

In the following sections, we will examine research questions that *do not work* for a generic qualitative dissertation, and questions that *do work* for a generic qualitative dissertation.

Research questions that are unsuitable for a generic qualitative dissertation

Yes or no questions

A research question will not work for a qualitative study if it requires a yes/no answer. The research question needs to elicit a description of experience and not require a yes/no answer.

Example of a yes or no question

Do men in male dominated occupations display discrimination toward women?

Explanation
A yes or no question lacks the qualitative stance; it does not aim to understand how individuals construct meaning from their experiences. This question will not lead to gathering descriptive data from the participant, and therefore, this question is not seeking a deeper understanding or discovery. This question cannot be answered by using qualitative methods and procedures.

Questions with preconceived ideas or pre-understandings
In the qualitative approach, the researcher sets aside preconceived ideas and pre-understandings. It is recommended that after developing the initial literature review, and prior to the data collection process, the researcher writes down everything they know about the topic. Setting aside preconceived ideas helps decrease researcher bias and facilitates respect for the uniqueness of each participant's experience. The researcher seeks to come from a position of not knowing in order to stay open to deeper understandings and discovery.

Example of a question with preconceived ideas
How do soldiers use support systems, family, and spirituality to cope with adjusting after returning from deployment?

Explanation
This question indicates that the researcher has preconceived ideas that soldiers use support systems, family, and spirituality to cope with adjustment after returning from deployment. By using support systems, family, and spirituality in the research question, the researcher limits the participants' descriptions of their experience. These preconceived ideas should be set aside. Investigating the entire experience would yield a fuller and richer description.

Having specific coping experiences stated in the research question also reduces the probability of discovery. Since the researcher has identified what they believe are innate in the coping experience, it will influence the data collected and the results of the analysis are then predisposed to researcher bias. The researcher thus loses the opportunity to capture the participants' holistic descriptions of their personal experiences. As such the following is a better question: *How do soldiers experience and describe adjustment after returning from deployment?* Or, *How do soldiers describe coping strategies after returning from deployment?*

Cause and effect questions

A qualitative research question cannot contain or suggest a cause and effect relationship. You can study cause and effect questions when conducting a psychological experiment because you can control for extraneous variables. In a qualitative research design, the researcher has no controls for extraneous variables. Qualitative research isn't supposed to be used to study cause/effect and therefore not supposed to control for extraneous variables. Qualitative research is about understanding people's experiences.

Example of a cause and effect question

How does childhood sexual abuse affect adult interpersonal relationships?

Explanation

Adult interpersonal relationships can be affected by many extraneous variables, not just childhood sexual abuse. In a qualitative study, the researcher cannot account for other variables that could impact adult interpersonal relationships.

Note

This question is not only attempting to study a cause and effect relationship, it presupposes that childhood sexual abuse affects adult interpersonal relationships. This research question may also have ethical concerns due to the possibility of traumatization.

There is potential of re-traumatizing the participant by eliciting memories of childhood sexual abuse. Overall, this question is inappropriate for a qualitative study.

Questions that require a measurement
The data from the qualitative procedures entail word descriptions. Tests and measurements are not used as data.

Example of a measurement needed to answer the research question
How does exercise improve depression?

Explanation
In order to answer this question, the improvement requires a measurement. Qualitative procedures cannot be used to measure improvements.

Note
This is also a cause and effect question with preconceived ideas. The researcher is alluding to the hypothesis that exercise does improve depression.

Questions involving vulnerable populations
"Do no harm" is the Hippocratic Oath taken by physicians and is a good lead to follow when a topic requires interviewing people who fit into the categories depicted by Institutional Review Boards (IRB) as vulnerable populations. There are many possible populations that might be considered vulnerable. Some examples of populations that the IRB may consider vulnerable are prisoners who could perceive that they *must* participate, or people with diminished capacity who lack the capability to consent.

Example question using a vulnerable population
How do women describe being victims of domestic violence?

Explanation

An IRB may not approve this topic. This question has a high potential for re-traumatization.

Note

Consider adjusting the research phenomenon to recovery. How do women describe the recovery process after leaving an abusive relationship?

Questions that create ethical complications

There are ethical considerations in questions that use deception or could result in social service or legal interventions.

Example question with ethical complications

What is the experience of elderly victims of abuse and neglect by their caretakers?

Explanation

The interview has potential for learning information that will require the researcher to report the incident to protective services (duty to warn and duty to protect).

Note

This question also has potential for emotional responses and re-traumatization.

Questions that will complicate recruiting

A dissertation research question that asks participants to admit and share information that is immoral, unethical, or illegal will create recruitment problems. Keep in mind that if you have no participants, you have no dissertation. These topics may also be placed under scrutiny by an IRB, making it difficult to obtain university approval.

Example question seeking to describe unethical behavior
What is the experience of being a middle school bully?

Explanation
This research question calls for middle school bullies to volunteer to be interviewed about their bullying behavior. There is a good possibility that bullies will not want to be interviewed.

A minor needs parental consent in order to be interviewed. Obtaining parental consent may add more complications to the recruitment process.

Note
There would be questions about whether middle school bullies would be honest during the interview on this topic. There are ethical concerns that could arise during the interview related to "duty to warn and duty to protect" adding to the list of possible problems with this dissertation topic.

Research questions with impractical timelines for completing a dissertation
Impractical timelines can hinder completing a dissertation. Some things to avoid specifically for a dissertation are longitudinal studies, topics that require too much time commitment from the participants, and topics that rely on other professionals to assist with your research.

When a research plan involves interviewing participants over time, you face the problem of participants dropping out of the study and having to recruit new participants. For example, you want to understand the process of recovery from addiction. You develop a research plan that requires interviewing eight participants during the first week of a 30-day treatment program. There is a short interview at mid-point. A third interview is conducted at the completion of the program. There is a weekly aftercare group for a month and then a final interview. This would be an interesting and relevant research plan if it was not for a dissertation. The researcher is asking for an unrealistic commitment from participants when on a dissertation time frame.

Possible problems
1. The treatment program which originally liked the idea of the study finds the interviews intrusive, interfering with their program.
2. Participants who originally volunteered to be part of the study drop out of treatment.
3. Participants decide to drop out of the research and do not complete the agreed upon interviews.
4. Participants do not show up for the final interview.

For every participant who does not complete the interviews, the researcher will need to recruit new participants who are beginning the program. The bottom-line is that you want a topic and research plan that does not include complications that could hinder the completion of your dissertation.

Questions addressing a psychological construct

We suggest avoiding research questions that include psychological constructs (e.g. self-esteem, attachment styles, defense mechanism, self-efficacy). Psychological constructs have already been defined and explained in the literature, which makes it difficult for the qualitative researcher who seeks understanding and discovery. The researcher takes the risk of conducting an extensive dissertation that reveals only what is already known. However, for the brave researchers who wish to address a psychological construct, they will need to first deconstruct the psychological construct to determine its underlying assumptions. According to Patton (2002), deconstruction means "to take apart the language of a text to expose its critical assumptions and ideological interests being served" (p. 101). By deconstructing the psychological construct, the researcher can develop a research question that addresses the critical assumptions and ideological interests.

Say, for example, the topic is burnout among home-based therapists. The initial research question is, *How do home-based therapists experience and describe burnout?* In reviewing numerous definitions of burnout in the literature, the researcher arrives at a summative definition that burnout refers to physical, mental, and emotional exhaustion induced by prolonged stressful work conditions (Golden et al., 2004).

If the researcher defines burnout for the participant, the researcher then runs the risk of biasing the study. Since generic qualitative research seeks to understand human experience, the researcher must set the context in which it is possible that a psychological construct could be experienced. The research question transforms from *How do home-based therapists experience and describe burnout?* to *What is the experience of working under prolonged stressful work conditions for home-based therapists?*

The process of developing a generic qualitative research question

> The researcher's greatest contribution perhaps is in working the research questions until they are just right.
>
> (Stake, 1995, pp. 19–20)

The qualitative generic research question is broad as compared to the quantitative research question. For students who were previously raised in the quantitative paradigm, it can be a challenge to evolve your thinking from narrow to openness. The qualitative research question addresses either experience or perception based on experience. The research question must be applicable to qualitative methodology. It is a single question that concentrates on what the student really wants to know. The question is drawn from the topic and clearly names the phenomenon under investigation.

You may think about the research question as sequential. Many qualitative questions follow a process, considering that experience inherently is composed of a past, present, and future. Take, for example, the question, *How do high achieving students describe academic success in community college?* The past brought the person to community college. The present describes current academic thinking, methods, and procedures, which leads to what academic success means for this person's future.

Creating the research question usually occurs over time. As the dissertation researcher immerses into the chosen topic, how to word the research question begins to take on a form. This process transpires from reading materials on the topic; seeking conversations with others about the topic; identifying through a review of the literature what is known about the topic, what is not known about the topic; and eventually, gaining the insight into what the researcher truly wants to know.

The evolution of the qualitative research question
In this section, we will observe the process of how two researchers worked with revising their research questions until the questions were appropriate for a generic qualitative dissertation and could be investigated using qualitative methods and procedures.

Evolution of the research question for researcher A
Researcher A wants to understand the how immigrants entering the United States navigate the acculturation process. The initial question developed was: *What qualities do adult immigrants in the United States describe as being effective resources for successful acculturation?*

In this question, the topic is successful acculturation among immigrants to the United States. The phenomenon under inquiry is effective resources. The population is adults who have experienced successful acculturation. Having the phenomenon under inquiry as effective resources will not produce rich qualitative data. The data collected may produce a list of effective resources instead of descriptive narrative data that describe experiences.

The evolved question is broad, holistic, and open to a deeper understanding and discovery. *How do adult immigrants experience and describe the process of acculturation?*

In the revised question, the topic is acculturation. The phenomenon under inquiry is the process of acculturation. The population is adults who have experienced acculturation. The revised question offers the potential for holistic understanding and is able to address all aspects of the experience.

Evolution of the research question for researcher B

In the second example, researcher B wants to know what psychological problems are experienced by male caregivers providing care to an elderly parent. The question began as: *What psychological problems are experienced by male caregivers providing care to an elderly parent?*

This question needs to be revised because it presents the problem of recruiting males with psychological problems caring for an elderly parent. Men with psychological problems could be under the category of a vulnerable population and would complicate IRB approval. Recruitment might be challenging because male participants are being asked to describe their psychological problems related to caregiving, which may not be a topic that a male caregiver would feel comfortable sharing with a stranger.

The first evolution to the above question was: *How do male caregivers describe their feelings about providing care to an elderly parent?* In this question, the topic is male caregivers. The phenomenon under inquiry is male's feelings about caretaking. The population is males who have feelings related to being a caregiver to an elderly parent. This question limits the experience of caretaking to feelings and does not address the experience in a holistic manner.

The third question which evolved by examining what the researcher wanted to understand and how to develop a question that was appropriate for a qualitative dissertation. <u>The evolution process produced a question that was broad, holistic, and open to a deeper understanding and discovery.</u> *How do adult males describe the experience of being a caregiver for an elderly parent?*

In the revised question, the topic is a male's experience of being a caregiver to an elderly parent. The phenomenon under inquiry is the experience of being a caregiver. The population is adult males who have experienced being a caregiver to an elderly parent. The revised question will explore the entire experience which might also embrace feelings as part of the caregiver's experience, but only if the participant describes feelings as part of his experience.

Other considerations during the evolution of the research question

The evolution of most generic dissertation research questions is towards openness and a holistic experience. However, it is appropriate to limit a topic by age, sex, culture, vocation, etc., when there is a rationale for using a specific population. In the question about immigrants' acculturation experience, naming a population of a specific culture would be appropriate. However, in the dissertation section that discusses the significance of the research topic, there needs to be a rationale for the specific culture the researcher is proposing to investigate. The rationale for a specific population would be provided by referencing academic material from your literature review that supports the use of a specific population. For a specific example, the question, *How do adult males describe the experience of being a caregiver for an elderly parent?*, the specific population would be supported by the literature revealing that the majority of caregiving studies has been based on female-caregivers and that there is currently an increase in male-caregivers.

Defining the terms of the research question

Once the research question has been developed, the researcher must define the terms of the question, preferably using references from the academic literature. This is important because many terms have multiple definitions and the researcher needs to accurately define the meaning of the terms used in the research question. This allows the researcher and the participant to clearly understand the meaning of the research question being explored.

Now that you have developed the research question and defined the terms of the question; your next step will be exploring methods and procedures used for a generic qualitative dissertation. Although recruitment will not occur until your topic, question, and dissertation research plan are approved by your academic institution, it is necessary to find out if you will be able to obtain participants for your dissertation. Some reasonable strategies must be in place for the time when you are ready to recruit participants for your study. Chapter 3 addresses the procedures necessary for a thoughtful recruitment plan and discusses ethical concerns, confidentiality, privacy, and protection for both the participants and the researcher.

Research plan

When you have selected a topic and developed a research question, it is time to examine the procedures necessary to develop your dissertation research plan. This chapter includes information for defining your population and the sampling strategy, and it includes a discussion on recruitment of participants. Confidentiality, ethical considerations, and gathering demographic information are also covered. The guidelines described in this chapter apply to the generic qualitative dissertation.

Population

The population of a study refers to all the possible persons eligible to be in the study. To stipulate who would be eligible to participate in the study, the researcher defines the inclusion criteria. The inclusion criteria are the characteristics that potential participants must possess in order to be included in the study. The inclusion criteria are constructed based on the traits and experience needed in order to answer the research question.

In qualitative research, a standard criterion is that participants must have had the experience of the phenomenon under inquiry

DOI: 10.4324/9781003195689-3

and be able to verbalize a description of their experiences. Other inclusion criteria are dependent on the research question. The inclusion criteria might include age, gender, education, and geographic location. For example, *How do adult males describe the experience of being a caregiver for an elderly parent?* The inclusion criteria for this research question might be adult males who have had the experience of being a caregiver for an elderly parent for a period of six months or more. Adding the time frame is a way of making sure the potential participant has had the experience for enough time to be able to answer the research question.

Sample

The sample is recruited from the population. The sample in a study refers to the participants who met the inclusion criteria and who are actually participating in the study. In a generic qualitative dissertation, the people who have been recruited and have agreed to be involved in the study are called participants.

Sample size

There are no rules for sample size in qualitative inquiry. Sample size depends on what you want to know, the purpose of the inquiry, what's at stake. What will be useful? What will have credibility, and what can be done with available time and resources?

(Patton, 2002, p. 244)

Sample size will vary depending on the nature of the topic and the manner by which data will be collected. For a generic qualitative dissertation, if the data collection procedure is individual interviews, the recommended sample size is 8–15 participants.

The range of the sample size may vary if the researchers are using multiple data collection methods which would increase the amount of data collected. Of most importance is that the researcher needs enough data to answer the research question. The overall goal is to collect quality data – substantial, meaningful, and rich. We will continue discussing data collection in more detail in Chapters 4 and 5.

Data saturation

A common practice in qualitative research is that the researcher might reduce the sample size if enough data are collected to reach data saturation. Data saturation is a term commonly linked to grounded theory studies. Charmaz (2014) stated, "Categories are 'saturated' when gathering fresh data no longer sparks new theoretical insights, nor reveals new properties of these core theoretical categories" (p. 213). Data saturation may occur during the data collection process, when the researcher perceives that no new information is being added. At this point the data being collected seems repetitive and redundant. The researcher claims that the data contain no new ideas and additional data are unlikely to generate any new ideas towards answering the research question.

However, there has been controversy based on the lack of guidelines to determine if data saturation has been achieved (Bowen, 2008). Bowen claimed, "The argument advanced in this research note is that claims of saturation should be supported by an explanation of how saturation was achieved and substantiated by clear evidence of its occurrence" (p. 117).

In our experience of chairing and serving on dissertation committees, it is best not to stop collecting data too soon because of the belief that you have reached data saturation. We question the statement, "additional data is unlikely to generate any new ideas towards answering the research question". Inexperienced researchers can have a false sense of data saturation because it is easier to find patterns and themes that are pre-understandings or characteristics that are already known about the topic. Thus, possibility of missing new discoveries because of a premature belief that no new ideas will arise from the data analysis.

Sampling strategy

Purposeful sampling "is the primary sampling strategy used in qualitative research" (Creswell, 2018, p. 318), and by extension is the sampling strategy used in the generic qualitative approach. Using purposeful sampling means recruiting participants who have had the experience under inquiry and are willing to describe their experience.

> Because the goal of qualitative research is enriching the understanding of an experience, it needs to select fertile exemplars of the experience for study. Such selections are purposeful and sought out; the selection should not be random or left to chance. The concern is not how much data were gathered or from how many sources but whether the data that were collected are sufficiently rich to bring refinement and clarity to understanding an experience.
> (Polkinghorne, 2005, p. 140)

Participant recruitment

Participant recruitment is the procedure by which the researcher recruits participants for the study. Recruitment normally consists of advertising for study participants, which usually occurs by displaying posters in public building such as schools, churches, doctors' offices, and libraries, or placing advertisements in a newspaper, newsletter, a journal, or advertising on the radio. In most cases, the researcher must obtain permission to advertise in order to recruit participants for the study. It is useful to check with your committee and IRB for guidelines on the need for obtaining permission. In all recruitment activities, participants who are interested in participating in the study will be asked to contact the researcher by a password-protected cell phone or password-protected email.

The use of social media has also become a popular recruiting tool. Facebook, Twitter, LinkedIn, and Google are rich recruitment grounds. Social media recruitment offers access to a broader pool of potential participants. The criteria for recruitment on social media vary by media site. Recruiting via social media is a new(ish) trend, not one that has evolved (or been altered) over a period of time. Recent concerns about personal privacy and confidentiality have altered social media permission on allowing certain topics of research recruitment. It is the responsibility of the researcher to investigate the requirements for recruiting on social media and to obtain permission if needed. The dissertation student should consult with their dissertation committee and the institution's IRB for guidance.

Ethical considerations

> In the history of social and medical science, there have been a few research studies that seriously injured people, and many more in which their welfare was not sufficiently protected.
>
> (Stake, 2010, p. 206)

APA Ethics Code

Ethical considerations are an essential part of human science research. Several ethical considerations must be considered in a generic qualitative dissertation. The APA Ethics Code offers standards for professional conduct and moral principles. The purpose of codes of conduct are to protect *research participants*. We suggest exploring this professional site during the beginning of planning your research. The APA standards are written and *periodically revised*. See https://www.apa.org/ethics/code for current descriptions of ethical principles and codes of conduct.

The APA standards for the recruitment process require that the purpose of the research is clearly articulated. The recruitment material must describe in detail what is expected of the participants in terms of the time commitment and the activities required for participation (interviewing, journaling, focus groups, etc.). The researcher must obtain informed consent forms from participants to participate in the study. The informed consent form must specify the information to be collected, how the information will be used, and how the information will be stored. It is important for the researcher not to try to influence potential participants to be involved in the study, and to inform potential participants that they can drop out of the study at any time without pressure or consequences.

The Institutional Review Board (IRB)
Another participant recruitment resource is your institution's IRB. If you have questions or concerns about ethics, your institution's IRB is the appropriate place for a consultation. It is essential to obtain IRB approval before beginning your research. Making sure you have identified and addressed any ethical concerns will benefit your process of obtaining IRB approval.

Attending to confidentiality, privacy, and protection
The researcher must develop a detailed description of confidentiality, privacy, and protection measures in the dissertation research plan, which also includes how safety is ensured for both the participants and the researcher. The researcher needs to consider whether there are any risks to study participants. The researcher is responsible for ensuring confidentiality, privacy,

and protection. Deception on any level is not used in a generic qualitative dissertation.

To protect privacy and confidentiality, both the researcher's and the participants' email accounts and phones must be password protected. The interviews must be held in a safe and private environment. Participants need to be aware that interviews are audio recorded. The researcher clarifies confidentiality and privacy procedures for collecting data. (This will vary depending on the sensitivity of the topic.) The data must be stored in a secure place.

Dual relationships

One common issue for the researcher is avoiding dual relationships with participants. A dual relationship in human science research is considered when multiple roles exist between a researcher and a participant. A dual relationship could occur when a person volunteers to participate in the dissertation study, and the researcher has a preexisting relationship with this person. For example, the researcher is employed as an Adjunct Professor at a community college and is recruiting participants for a dissertation study on the experience of the transition during the first year of college. There are a few concerns to consider for preventing an ethical concern created by a dual relationship:

- A student may anticipate their grades being impacted by the choice to participate or not participate.
- A past student may volunteer to be in the study because they received an A grade in a previous course taught by the researcher and feels obligated to participant.
- A student may be planning to enroll in a future course taught by the researcher and perceives that it will be advantageous for her grade if they volunteer.

The researcher wants to avoid situations in which the potential participant may feel obligated to participate in the study. However, these examples presented may not create an ethical concern if the participant is assured that it is their decision to participate in the study and is informed that they can drop out of the study at any time.

The researcher needs to consider the potential of whether the interview could include personal or delicate information and may cause embarrassment for the student. The researcher wants to avoid an uncomfortable situation that could negatively affect the participant's college experience.

A possible suggestion might be *not* to recruit from the community college in which the researcher is employed. The researcher might consider seeking permission to recruit from other community colleges in the area. If you have any questions or concerns about a possible ethical dilemma, it is always best to check with your dissertation committee and the IRB.

Demographics information

During recruitment of the sample, the researcher gathers demographic information. It is required information in order to be able to present the description of the sample in your dissertation. The demographics of the sample must be relevant toward understanding the topic under inquiry. Common demographic information could consist of name, sex, race, and age range. You may not ask for demographic information if it is not relevant to the topic and the research question under inquiry.

As an example, recall the previous research question about how males describe the experience of being a caregiver for an elderly parent. The demographic information that could be relevant towards understanding the experience includes the age of the caretaker, the age of the parent, the length of time the male participant has been a caretaker, and possibly race and marital status, as well as whether the participant works full- or part-time, or is a live-in caregiver. These demographics may add meaning to your findings. For this research topic, you would not need to collect demographic information such as educational status, religion, or geographical area because these demographics are not relevant to answering the research question.

In a qualitative generic dissertation, we suggest the use of a face sheet to collect demographics prior to the interview, but not as part of the interview process. The face sheet could be emailed to participants with the intention of it being completed and handed in before the interview begins. The demographics face sheet should *not* be collected at the starting point of the interview because it could set the tone for the interview as a question and answer session. Instead, you want to start the interview by exploring the phenomenon under inquiry as a conversational tone or a dialogue.

Once the sample has been established, the next step in a generic qualitative dissertation is data collection. Chapter 4 will address developing the main research question and how to create open-ended interview questions. It will also examine data collection using interviews.

Preparing for the interview

The most recommended manner of collecting data in a generic qualitative dissertation is through face-to-face, audio-recorded, in-depth, semi-structured interviews or conversational interviews. In both the semi-structured and conversational interviews, the guiding interview questions should be open-ended and designed to open the semantic space of the interview.

The conversational interview is dependent on the style of the interviewer. During the conversational interview, the researcher follows the participant's lead. Polkinghorne (2005) explained that "The conversation consists of a give and take dialectic in which the interviewer follows the conversational trends opened up by the interviewee and guides the conversation toward producing a full account of the experience under investigation" (p. 142). Some researchers are comfortable with the conversational interview. Others may find their comfort zone with the semi-structured interview. Both interviews are appropriate for a generic qualitative study.

The guiding interview questions should encourage descriptions of the participants' lived experience. "In stark contrast to structured interviewing, qualitative interviewing is flexible and dynamic" (Taylor & Bogdan, 1998, p. 88). The interview

DOI: 10.4324/9781003195689-4

questions should not require answers that are true or false, yes or no, or multiple choice. The interview should not proceed like a survey or a question/answer session. The guiding interview questions are not used in as rigid a manner as one might do in a survey. The researcher strives to construct interview questions that create an atmosphere that facilitates an open dialogue.

The purpose of creating a set of relevant guiding interview questions is because they can assist an inexperienced researcher with facilitating the interviewing process. If the participant stops talking and looks for guidance from the interviewer, having prepared guiding questions helps keep the conversation moving. It is not uncommon for a participant to get off track during the interview. The prepared guiding interview questions can assist with bringing the dialogue back to the topic.

Prepared guiding questions must be drawn from the research question with no new material introduced. The interviewer must be careful to "avoid leading the witness". If a participant brings up something new, the interviewer may pursue it, but only if it is relevant to the topic under inquiry.

The generic qualitative interview is primarily about the participant's perceptions and experiences related to the topic under inquiry. Taylor and Bogdan (1998) stated that one aspect of the virtue of the interview is that the person being interviewed gains "new insights and understandings of their experiences" (p. 98). As the person being interviewed is exploring their experiences, the possibility increases for gaining a deeper understanding about their experiences. The interviewer facilitates this process by asking probing or clarifying questions, but with some caution. The researcher stays aware of not over-stepping the boundaries of the interview topic. The insights gained and shared by the interviewee add depth and meaning to the data collected.

Bogdan and Taylor (1975) depicted the reasons for avoiding forced-choice questions. "By asking structured or forced-choice questions initially, the researcher creates a mind-set in informants about the right or wrong things to say that can make it difficult if not impossible to get at how they really see things" (p.102). The researcher seeks to create guiding interview questions that facilitate openness. Learning to create open-ended interview questions is a thoughtful procedure. Charmaz (2006) emphasized the benefits of creating open-ended interview questions: "Simply thinking through how to word open-ended questions averts forcing responses into narrow categories" (p. 18).

The first question can be a revised version of the research question. This question allows the participant to tell their story. As Charmaz (2006) wrote, "Your first question may suffice for the whole interview if stories tumble out. Receptive 'un huhs' a few clarifying questions or comments may keep a story coming when a participant can and wants to tell it" (p. 29). If the participant shares their story at the beginning of the interview, the researcher listens, and if needed, facilitates by paraphrasing and using probing questions. Only when the participant stops will the researcher select a guiding interview question that has not already been addressed to move the interview along.

The relationship between the research topic, dissertation title, research question, and the guiding interview questions: maintaining the alignment

It is important that your topic, dissertation title, research question, and guiding interview questions are consistent with each other and flow together! The alignment of the topic, title, research question, and guiding questions provide the reader of the dissertation a manner by which they can see the flow of data from the research question, through data collection, analysis, and the presentation of the findings of the study. It is important in a dissertation for the reader to see the process of developing and completing the study. The alignment between topic, research question, and interview questions helps create credibility and trustworthiness because the reader can see that that the researcher was investigating what they claimed to investigate.

Therefore, when developing your guiding interview questions, they must be aligned with the interview topic and focused on answering the research question. It is important that your guiding questions be derived from the research question. Asking a question that is not related to the research question results in leading the participant. Also, asking questions outside the boundaries of your research question may not be consistent with the participant's experience. If researchers ask questions that are off track, they will end up with a great deal of unusable data because the data will not be related to answering the research question. If you ask questions that are too leading, your data will reflect researcher bias. If you ask "why" questions, you will get rationalizations instead of descriptions of experience.

In summary, ask only open-ended, probing, and clarifying questions that are aligned with the research question. When the interview questions are misaligned, this tends to muddy the data. Ensuring that your interview questions align with the research question contributes to the trustworthiness of data collected during the interview.

The use of probing and clarifying questions are essential during the qualitative interview. The probing and clarifying questions are impartial, keeping the alignment focused on answering the research question. Examples of probing or clarifying questions are shown here:

- That is interesting. Can you tell me more about...?
- What did that mean to you?
- How did you handle the problem of...?

- What happened after...?
- How was the issue resolved?
- How did that make you feel?
- Can you give me an example of...?

Developing guiding interview questions and maintaining the alignment

We have discussed preparing open-ended guiding interview questions and keeping the interview question in alignment with the topic, title, and the research question. Below are three examples of how to create guiding interview questions that are open-ended and keep the alignment.

Topic: expressing will
Title: The Experience of Expressing Will
Research question: What is the experience of expressing will?
Data collected: A conversational interview and a journal focused on the experience of expressing will.

Guiding interview questions:

1. Please describe your experience of expressing will in as much detail as possible.
2. What have you discovered from your journal about yourself, and how you express will?
3. What are your feelings connected with expressing will?
4. What are your thoughts connected with expressing will?
5. How would you describe any physical or bodily responses during the experience of expressing will?
6. What precipitates your expression of will?
7. What stops you from expressing your will?
8. Is there anything important in your experience of expressing will that we have not discussed?

Topic: romantic love

Title: The Experience of Romantic Love

Research question: What is the experience of romantic love?

Data collected: Individual conversational interviews

 Guiding interview questions:

1. How would you describe your experience of romantic love within your relationship?
2. What allows you to know you are in romantic love?
3. What is it like to experience romantic love?
4. Please describe a time of experiencing romantic love that stands out for you.
5. How would you describe your feelings when experiencing romantic love?
6. Is there anything we have not discussed that would be important for me to know about your experience of romantic love?

Topic: recovery from opiate prescription drugs

Title: The Process of Recovery from Opiate Prescription Drugs

Research Question: How do adults describe the process of recovery from dependence on opiate prescription drugs?

Data collection: Semi-structured individual interviews

 Guiding interview questions:

1. Please describe your process of recovery in as much detail as possible starting with the first day of your recovery.
2. What is it like to be in recovery?
3. What has been helpful towards facilitating your recovery?
4. What has been your biggest challenge during your recovery?
5. How would you describe any changes that have promoted recovery?
6. Is there anything that we have not discussed that would be important for me to know in order to better understand your recovery process?

We previously discussed the reasons for not asking questions that are outside the boundaries of your research question. The research question on the process of recovery from dependence on opiate prescription drugs provides a good example of staying aware of keeping focused on the research question. The interview questions stayed focused on recovery. There were no interview questions about drug-using behavior during the participant's active use of opiate drugs. Asking a question about drug-using behavior or what brought the participant into recovery is outside the boundaries of the research question. The participant has signed a consent form to be involved in your study on recovery. Therefore, it is unethical to interview on any topic other than what was described in the consent form. However, if during the interview the participant compares progress in recovery with their using behavior, then awareness of changes may be part of the recovery process and should be included in the data as part of the experience.

The final interview question in each of the above examples checks to make sure that the participant is able to share any information that was not included in the interview questions. As the interview progressed, it might have facilitated further self-reflection. Asking the participant to share information that was not asked during the interview may provide the participant the opportunity to share any new insights gained during the interview and provides a closure to the interview process.

Interviewing protocol

The persona of the interviewer is relaxed, nonjudgmental, sensitive, respectful, and patient. The interviewer sets the stage by being a "cheerful data collector" (Taylor & Bogdan, 1998, p. 88). Patton (2015) described a good interview as one in which a connection is formed, and the conversation is flowing both ways.

The interviewer attempts to create an atmosphere that is comfortable for promoting open communication. The interviewer's concern is a quiet, comfortable, and safe setting. The setting chosen for the interview should ensure confidentiality for the participant. Interviews in restaurants, public parks, and shopping malls do not provide confidentiality because the interview could be overheard. A good choice for conducting a qualitative interview is a private office in a public library. The public library is available to members of the community, so entering the setting does not directly identify the interviewee as a research participant. Library patrons occupying the library makes the setting public enough to provide security for both the interviewer and interviewee.

The best environment for the interview is face-to-face; however, when a private physical space is not possible, the interview can be conducted using Skype or the telephone. However, there is always the potential problem for interruptions during the interview when using Skype or phone interviews because there is not adequate control of the interview environment.

Members of vulnerable populations are an exception to this mode of interviewing. We do not recommend using Skype or telephone when interviewing participants who are members of a vulnerable population. However, whether to use Skype or telephone interviews is a decision that is best discussed with your dissertation committee and the IRB.

Finally, the researcher should be certain that the participant understands confidentiality and signs a consent form to participate in the study. All manners of interviews should be audio recorded and transcribed before the data analysis begins. It is recommended that the interview is not only audio recorded, but that the researcher should use two audio-recording devices to avoid losing the interview data due to equipment failure.

Other qualitative data collection methods

While interviews are the most common means of collecting data in a generic qualitative dissertation, other qualitative data collection methods are compatible to use in combination with individual interviews. The generic qualitative approach allows for flexibility in data collection and supports the use of triangulation of data sources. Triangulation means using more than one source of collecting data on the topic under inquiry. When gathering data from more than one source in a dissertation, the researcher analyzes the data from each source and compares the results. The purpose of using more than one way to collect data is for identifying consistencies in the data. Triangulation is a procedure that strengthens trustworthiness of your research findings.

In this chapter we will explore other appropriate and creative ways to collect data. These procedures will be explored to specify what constitutes data, and to discuss how to apply other ways of collecting data for a generic qualitative dissertation, with specific attention to practical timelines for completing the dissertation.

DOI: 10.4324/9781003195689-5

Focus groups

Focus groups are used to collect data from a small group of people in a guided discussion on a specific topic. Berg and Lune (2012) suggested small groups of no more than seven participants as larger groups are harder to control and tend to break up into smaller groups.

In focus groups, the researcher leads the discussion on a specific topic and facilitates discussion. The researcher encourages discussion among the participants. The focus group interaction allows the participants to explore the experiences of the topic under inquiry through the group interaction. The focus group interactions have potential for obtaining a deeper and broader perspective of the topic. For a generic qualitative dissertation, we suggest the focus group is used in a sequence with individual interviews.

Focus group sessions after individual interviews

The timing of the focus group in the dissertation research plan is dependent on the research topic. For certain topics, it may be productive to begin with a focus group and conduct individual interviews afterwards. As an example, consider a focus group investigating learning experiences with students who have learning disabilities. Conducting individual interviews a week after the focus group session potentially provides participants with time to process the discussions that occurred during the focus group. Allowing time for processing of the discussions serves as a way to increase the participant's awareness of their own experiences that have promoted learning. Therefore, having the individual interview after the focus group session may provide additional comprehensions to the data collected during the focus group.

Focus group sessions prior to individual interviews

There are also reasons for having individual interviews completed prior to a focus group. Using a different example, a study on recovery from gastric bypass surgery could begin with individual accounts about the process of recovery through semi-structured or conversational interviews. After completing data collection and analysis of the individual interviews, a focus group session consisting of the participants in your study could be arranged for the purpose of discussion about the findings from data analyzed from the individual interviews.

During the focus group, the researcher presents the interpretations of the findings from the individual interviews and asks for feedback from the participants. The researcher initiates a conversation on the findings. The discussion on the findings provides the opportunity for adding data and insights into the initial analysis. In the case that participants agree and support your findings, the focus group could serve as a validity check.

Advantages of focus groups

Focus groups are a convenient and economic usage for gathering large amounts of data in a short period of time (Boateng, 2012). The researcher prepares open-ended interview questions that will draw out information and creates an atmosphere that supports open and frank discussions. As the researcher gathers data from the participants in the group, the researcher has the advantage of listening to multiple perspectives made possible by the dialogue between the participants. According to Berg and Lune (2012), "Most importantly, focus groups allow researchers to observe interactions and discussions among the informants" (p. 166). Group members are encouraged to agree or to disagree, to offer different perspectives, and to debate issues. The strength of the focus group is the lack of restrictions for discussing different points of view, along with being able to validate feelings and perspectives, and explore new ideas.

Disadvantages of focus groups

It is not advised to use focus groups when the research question addresses potentially sensitive or embarrassing content. Participants may feel uncomfortable sharing sensitive or embarrassing experiences in front of others. Participants may take a "hold back" attitude (Boateng, 2012, p. 55) because they do not know the other persons in the group.

On the contrary, a person might feel pressured to share, only to feel embarrassed afterwards. In focus groups used for research, it is the responsibility of the researcher to protect participants from unnecessary distress. Therefore, focus groups are counter indicated for some research topics.

Another limitation of the focus group is a construct known as *groupthink.* Irving Janis (1972) is credited with the theory on groupthink. Janis was well known for his studies on political policy decisions in which conformity led to faulty decision-making.

"Group think refers to a deterioration of mental efficiency, reality testing, and moral judgment that result from in-group pressure" (Janis, 1982, p. 9). It is necessary for a researcher to be aware of the possibility of social pressure leading to conformity when collecting data while facilitating focus group *discussions. In his article on the efficacy of focus group discussions,* Boateng (2012) states, "it is susceptible to the dangers groupthink may pose on individual participants responses, which can significantly impact on the outcome of studies" (p. 54).

Groupthink is identified during a focus group session when one or two of the participants take control of the group. These are individuals who perceive that they know more than anyone else in the room and dominate the group discussion. The results are that other group members are influenced by these group members' perceptions, or they react to the subgroup pressure by feeling uncomfortable with revealing their personal thoughts. Group members may also feel pressure to conform in order to keep the group cohesion. When groupthink dominates the focus group, it interferes with a researcher's ability to effectively gather useful and relevant data.

One way to address groupthink is to contact each person who participated in the group a day or two after the focus group session. The questions the researcher should ask are, is there anything you would like to add to the group discussion? Are there any perceptions or experiences that you did not have the opportunity to discuss during the group? After the group, were there new ideas that you thought about that related to (the topic under inquiry)? The follow-up phone conversation provides the opportunity for the participants to add their perspectives that they were unable to share during the focus group session. And it provides the researcher with additional data. How the researcher sets the ground rules will also help address the problems related to groupthink.

Setting up ground rules

The participants are made aware that the focus group session(s) are audio recorded and transcribed. At the beginning of the focus group, the researcher defines the purpose of the group and presents the guidelines. The guidelines should include turning off cell phones, limiting discussion to one person at a time, and showing respect for each person's point of view. It is made clear that confidentiality cannot be guaranteed; instead, the researcher encourages participants to respect confidentiality, and requests that what is said in the group stays in the group. The researcher explains that direct quotes from this focus group might be used in the dissertation; however, quotes will not be linked to a specific person.

Taylor and Bogdan (1998) state that the researcher's responsibility is "managing interactions between members of the group – for example, keeping people from interruption or arguing with each other, dealing with overly talkative people who would monopolize the conversation, encouraging shy people to contribute, and so on" (p. 113). As a way to guard against groupthink, the researcher is clear about the expectation that everyone will have the opportunity to share their perspective. The researcher explains that conversations may be interrupted in order to make sure that all participants are included, and each person is allotted time to share their viewpoints.

Facilitating the focus group

The researcher creates an environment that is nonjudgmental and open. It is repeated that everyone's input is considered valuable. The guiding interview questions are used to keep the discussion on track. The researcher uses probing questions to clarify meanings and to facilitate a deeper exploration of the topic under investigation.

An easel pad can be used to keep notes on the assorted viewpoints within the discussion. At various times, or during a lull in the conversation, the researcher reviews and summarizes the notes taken during the discussion. The researcher encourages feedback from the group. This will contribute to making sure the researcher is accurately interpreting the discussion.

The researcher's goal is to gather rich data. Personal sharing is encouraged and valued over intellectualizing or dialogue about another person's experience. Conversations based on personal experiences enhance the exploration toward understanding the meanings and essence of the topic under inquiry.

Journaling

The Intensive Journal is specifically designed to provide an instrument and techniques by which persons can discover within themselves the resources they did not know they possessed. It is to enable them to draw the power of deep contact out of the actual experiences of their lives so that they can recognize their own identity and harmonize it with the larger identity of the universe as they experience it.

(Progoff, 1975, p. 10)

Requesting or inviting participants to keep a journal of their experiences related to the topic under inquiry is an innovative procedure with the potential of adding depth and breadth to the data collected. The process of writing in a journal or diary entails the participant to both focus their attention on their experiences and organize how to record those experiences. The journaling process may consist of writing down key phrases or words that feel significant, while other journal entries may be extended and assist in focusing internally with the purpose of drawing meaning from their experiences.

Specific guidelines for a dissertation

Journaling as a way of collecting data has many advantages. If you ask your participants to journal prior to your interview it helps prepare the person for the interview. For some people writing is an easier way to express themselves compared to interviews. The participants are given the opportunity to immerse themselves into memories and thoughts related to the experience. The participant is not limited to the questions asked in the interview and the order in which the interview questions occur. For some, it may be a more dynamic approach leading to a deeper understanding of the meanings underlying the experience.

Journaling has a few shortcomings which could impede the timelines for your dissertation. The risk of a participant that was a prolific writer could result in 50 pages of a hand-written journal given to you, which may or may not stay focused on the topic under inquiry. It could be an extremely time-consuming process to sift through large amounts of data to determine depictions that answer the research question.

For the purpose seeking rich data with respect for the time restraints of a dissertation, one suggestion would be to request that the participants bring a synthesis of what they have learned from their journal to the interview session. This synthesis would be discussed during the interview, and the written synthesis would be analyzed as data, in the same way a transcribed interview would be analyzed.

Another option would be to ask the participant to keep a journal prior to the interview for the purpose of discussing the journal during the interview. The researcher would ask questions related to what the participant learned from keeping a journal. The researcher would ask clarifying questions as needed.

These two procedures are likely to enhance the interview without the problem of using excessive time for handling large amounts of data that may or may not relate to the research topic.

Open-ended questionnaires

Questionnaires can be used to collect qualitative data if the questionnaires are open-ended, *not* requiring true and false or multiple-choice answers. Questionnaires used in combination with focus groups or interviews can add to the richness of the data collected. In order to respond to the questionnaire, the participant must think about how they want to answer the questions, thus facilitating self-reflection. The advantage of open-ended questionnaires is that it allows the researcher to collect answers to the questions posed by the questionnaire which represent the actual words of the research participants. Another benefit of using questionnaires is that it allows the researcher to collect data in an organized timely manner.

Example questions used in a questionnaires

The following are sample questionnaire questions related to topics discussed earlier in this book:

1. Could you describe in your own words when you knew that you were in romantic love?
2. Please describe in your own words a time when you realized that you were expressing will?
3. Could you describe your thoughts and feelings during your first week in recovery from opiate drugs?

How to use questionnaires

The qualitative questionnaire works well in combination with either individual interviews or focus groups. If you are collecting data by using the questionnaire and an individual interview, the questionnaire would be collected from the participant prior to the individual interview. During the interview, you would begin by asking a question that is a version of your research questions. At an appropriate time during the interview, you would engage the participant in a dialogue relating to the participant's questionnaire answers. The use of probing or clarifying questions could expand on the questionnaire answers and add to the depth of the interview.

If you are collecting data using focus groups, you could use the qualitative questionnaire answers from all the participants to construct interview questions to be used during the focus groups. During the focus group the researcher uses these questions for the purpose of expanding on experiences that are deemed important in the participants' written descriptions revealed in the questionnaires.

Using qualitative questionnaires prior to individual interviews or prior to a focus group allows the participant time to reflect on thoughts or experiences related to the topic under inquiry. Thus, the combination of questionnaires and interviews and/or focus groups provides a triangulation of data source which adds to the trustworthiness of the data collected.

Personal documents

> The phrase 'personal documents' refer to individuals' written first-person accounts of their whole lives or parts of their lives, or their reflections on a specific event or topic.
>
> (Taylor & Bogdan, 1998, pp. 123–124)

In the previous sections about journaling and open-ended questionnaires, we have touched on the ways that narratives of personal documents can enhance the data collection process. Narratives provide a means for participants to immerse themselves in the experience. In most cases, participants writing about their experiences allow them to deliver a clearer more detailed description of their experience during the individual interview.

This section will explore other possibilities available for collecting rich and insightful narrative data through personal documents. Personal documents include, but are not limited to, diaries, sent or unsent letters, pictures, drawings, photos, poetry, and song lyrics.

When collecting data using pictures, drawings, photos, poetry, and song lyrics, the researcher asks the participants to bring the articles or documents to the interviews. The participants are asked for their interpretation of the data source. According to Merriam (1998) personal documents are a reliable source of data but because they are personal they are highly subjective, "the writer is the only one to select what he or she considers important to record" (p. 116). Therefore, the researcher asks specifically for a participant to describe what each article means to them and how it fits as an illustration regarding the topic under inquiry. The researcher listens and uses probing and clarifying questions as needed.

If it seems appropriate to the topic, the researcher asks the participants to bring any narratives with them to the interview that would illuminate their experience of the phenomenon under inquiry. Regarding the study on romantic love, this might include *letters* exchanged while apart, *photos* of special times, *song lyrics* identified as "our song", a *poem* describing the romantic relationship, etc.

With regard to the study on recovery, narratives might include *sent or unsent letters, or photos* that represent meaningful life activities that support recovery, or a *drawing or poetry* that portrays the person's feelings about recovery.

Field notes

Field notes are the researcher's thoughts throughout the data collection process and an important part of the data analysis. Writing field notes occurs after each interview or focus group. According to Taylor and Bogdan (1998), the interviewer records observations of gestures and non-verbal expressions that add to the meaning of the participant's words. The researcher also develops notes about their interpretations and hunches.

Field note protocol for interviews

The researcher stays fully present throughout the qualitative interview. Thus, field notes are written immediately following the interview. The researcher strives for authenticity, which can be facilitated when the atmosphere of the interview is experienced as a dialogue or conversation. Writing notes during an interview can interrupt the conversational flow of the interview.

Writing notes during the interview could also influence what information the participant shares with the interviewer. For example, imagine that the participant is expressing personal information with the interviewer. The eye contact with the interviewer lets the participant know that the interviewer is listening to what is being shared. Then the interviewer's attention wanders to the note pad on the interviewer's lap, and the interviewer begins writing. A common reaction would be curiosity about what the interviewer is writing. The participant may interpret the note writing as what the interviewer thinks is important to note and become more self-conscious of what he or she shares during the remainder of the interview. At this point the flow of the conversation has been interrupted, and it most likely will change the course of the interview. The course of the interview has been altered. It has changed the interviewee's self-reflective dialogue to an external interaction influenced by the note-taking behavior of the interviewer.

Writing field notes immediately following the interview allows the interviewer to remain fully focused on the participant's story throughout the interview. Taking notes after the interview facilitates writing field notes that are reflective of a holistic interpretation of the interview. The field notes taken after the interview include observational data, interpretations, or questions. Observations could include gestures, facial expressions, or other significant observations that would not be obvious in the audio-recorded transcript. Examples of observation are *the participant became tearful while sharing...., the participant twisted her hair between her fingers while talking about..., the participant stood up and paced during the discussion of...the participant continued to bring up...*

While writing field notes, the researcher makes interpretations regarding the relationship between the interview data and answering the research question. The researcher separates interpretations of the data by what is already known about the topic, what adds to the understanding of the topic, and what are possible new discoveries. Writing field notes about each interview helps the researcher in planning future interviews and interpreting data during the analysis process (Taylor & Bogdan, 1998).

Researcher bias

The researcher's field notes, which are reflections from the data collected, can also serve as a check for decreasing researcher bias. During the qualitative process of setting aside pre-understanding and preconceived ideas, the researcher seeks assurance that the interpretations within their field notes accurately represent the participant's descriptions of the experience under inquiry, and not the researcher's preconceived ideas.

Field notes protocol for focus groups

Field notes for the focus groups differ from the individual interviews because field notes are taken *during* the focus group. As stated earlier it is recommended to have an easel pad to be used for summarizing discussions throughout the group session. Therefore, the researcher takes notes on prominent ideas and differing viewpoints that will be shared with the group intermittently to facilitate further exploration. Thus, during the focus group, the group members realize that the notes taken by the researcher will be summarized for them for the purpose of further discussion and exploration of the topic under inquiry.

After the focus group session, the researcher writes field notes that describe observations of behaviors that would not be evident on the audio-recorded transcript. Overall, the purpose of the field notes is to help the researcher to identify questions, examine interpretations, and check for pre-understanding and researcher bias. The field notes are processed to enhance the data analysis.

Once the data are collected in a generic qualitative study, the next step is to conduct the data analysis using a thematic analysis process. Chapter 6 is the exciting part of the research: the data analysis process.

The investigator's role in qualitative research is compared to that of a detective. At first everything is important; everyone is suspect. It takes time and patience to search for clues, to follow up leads, to find the missing pieces, to put the puzzle together.

(Merriam, 1998, p. 21)

Data analysis is where imagination, creativity, and diligence make sense out of the meanings of the experience investigated.

Data analysis

This chapter offers guidance in the form of a step-by-step process for the data analysis appropriate for a generic qualitative dissertation. Thematic analysis is a respected data analysis procedure that has a long history of recognition in the social sciences. A thematic analysis can be used to carry out an analysis of qualitative data for most topics in the social sciences. It works well with data collected from interviews and other data that were described in Chapter 5. Braun and Clarke (2006) said, "thematic analysis involves the searching across a data set – be that a number of interviews or focus groups, or a range of texts – to find repeated patterns of meanings" (p. 86).

Understanding guidelines prior to beginning the data analysis

The data are analyzed through the lens of the main research question. Do not make the mistake of trying to analyze data by using the interview questions. Using your guiding questions will compartmentalize the data, preventing connections within the whole interview, and presenting the appearance of survey data.

DOI: 10.4324/9781003195689-6

When you analyze your data, you will use your main research question and will only use data that answer your main research question. Aronson (1994) described the focus of thematic analysis on "identifiable themes and patterns of living and/or behavior" (p. 1).

There may be interesting data that do not provide enough support for answering your research question. Keep a file of interesting data that are questionable for answering your research question. Check on this file later. The data and the researcher are interactive during the analysis process; therefore, intuitive connections are worth exploring.

A metaphor for qualitative analysis is a good mystery book. From both Sherlock Holmes and Hercule Poirot, we have learned not to theorize until gathering enough data. When you develop a theory too soon, you can make the mistake of trying to fit your data into your premature theory. You must keep *fresh eyes* throughout the entire analysis process.

Three types of thematic analysis will be described in this chapter: inductive analysis, theoretical analysis, and thematic analysis with constant comparison (CC). Deciding which model of thematic analysis to use depends on the research question and the research plan.

All three types begin with an initial line-by-line analysis coding or an incident-by-incident analysis coding. Line-by-line analysis involves sentences while incident-by-incident analysis involves two sentences to a paragraph describing the same meaning unit. This line-by-line procedure initially breaks down the text which will later be combined by clustering similar codes to develop patterns. The thinking during the initial coding is on action and meaning. What is happening here? What does it mean?

Use the participant's wording whenever possible, during the coding. Example taken from a transcript: "I was thinking that quite often the expression of will is something that starts with a struggle within me. Not so much something I feel outside of myself but an internal conflict". The initial coding was *internal conflict*. Using the participant's wording when coding the data is one way to capture the participant's meanings and decrease researcher bias. The codes may shift and will be modified during the analysis process; however, if you are starting with the participant's wording you will have a better chance of capturing the participant's experience and adding validity to your findings.

Thematic analysis

> Since this is an inductive and intuitive process, there are no simple procedures or techniques for this kind of analysis. You may find it helpful to ask yourself questions like: 'What do these quotes or observations have in common?' 'What's going on here?' 'What does this tell me about how people view their world?' How do these themes relate to each other?
>
> (Taylor & Bogdan, 1998, p. 156)

Inductive analysis

Inductive analysis (IA) is data driven and does not attempt to fit the data into any preexisting categories. The researcher attempts to set aside all pre-understandings and preconceived ideas. The data collected from each participant (interviews, journals, open-ended questionnaire, etc.) are analyzed individually. During this process the researcher immerses themselves into each participant's data individually.

Step-by-step analysis

1. Review and familiarize yourself with the data collected from the first participant (interviews, journals, field notes, records, documents, etc.). Read the documents and highlight intuitively any sentences, phrases, or paragraphs that appear to be meaningful.

2. Review the highlighted data, and use your research question to decide if the highlighted data are related to answering your question. Some information in the transcript may be interesting but does not relate to your question.

3. Set aside all highlighted data that are not related to your question. Create and label a separate file to store this data. You may want to come back and reevaluate these data in the future.

4. Data that are determined to be relevant to the research question are called meaning units. Meaning units consist of direct quotes from the transcribed interviews (or other narrative data). Create a code for each meaning unit.

5. Cluster the coded meaning units that are related or connected in some manner and begin your process of developing patterns. Note that the original coding may change as you determine names for each identified pattern.

6. Patterns are "what is happening?" As patterns are discovered, list meaning units under the related pattern. Read the quotes under each pattern. You want to make sure the quotes align with the pattern, and that the names of the patterns make sense.

7. Each pattern should be described and elucidated by supporting quotes from the data. Briefly describe each pattern and the relationship of the pattern to the research question.

8. Take all the patterns from your first transcript, and look for the emergence of overarching themes. This process involves combining and clustering the related patterns to create themes. "A theme captures something important about the data in relation to the research question and represents some level of patterned response of meaning within the data set" (Braun & Clarke, 2006, p. 80).

9. After all the data have been analyzed, arrange the themes to correspond with the supporting patterns. The patterns are listed under the theme. Each pattern is elucidated by direct

quotes from the transcript. The patterns are used to elucidate the themes.

10. For each theme, write a detailed analysis describing the
scope and substance of each theme.

11. Repeat this process for each participant's data.

12. Once the data from all participants have been analyzed,
the repeating patterns and themes from all participants
are synthesized together into a composite synthesis, which
attempts to interpret the meanings and/or implications
regarding the question under investigation.

Theoretical analysis

Theoretical analysis (ThA) is employed in a situation in which the
research has some predetermined categories (themes) to examine during the data analysis. In this situation, the researcher may
use their pre-understandings when conducting the data analysis.
However, in this case the researcher also remains open to the
possibilities of new themes emerging from the data during the
analysis.

Theoretical thematic analysis is driven by theory and themes
that are predetermined and should be addressed in the research
question. Take this question for example, what is the experience
of developing forethought and self-reflection when transition-
ing from high school to college among young adults? In this
case, the research question contains two concepts from theories
on human development: forethought and self-reflection. These
concepts are being drawn from Bandura's (2006) core properties of *agency*. Forethought and self-reflection are being used in
the research as predetermined themes.

The data collected are analyzed for each participant individually, and patterns that emerged from the data are organized
under the corresponding preexisting themes, keeping in mind
that new patterns and themes could also emerge during the data
analysis process.

Researchers might approach ThA in two phases: In phase one, after preparing the data (Steps 1–4 below), the researcher works on assigning the data meaning units to the predetermined themes early on and completes the analyses as described in Steps 5–13. Then, in phase two, the researcher returns to the data and works with data meaning units and patterns that did not seem to fit the predetermined categories, again following Steps 5–13. The themes derived from the second phase of analysis will likely not be found in previous research but may contribute to it.

Step-by-step analysis

1. Read, review, and familiarize yourself with the data collected from each participant (interviews, journals, field notes, records, documents etc.). Keeping the predetermined categories (themes) and the research question in mind, re-read the documents and highlight intuitively any sentences, phrases, or paragraphs that appear to be meaningful, as well as remaining open to any new patterns and themes that are related to the research question and have emerged from the data analysis. During this process, the researcher immerses themselves in each participant's data individually.

2. For each participant, review the highlighted data and use your research question to decide if the highlighted data are related to your question. Some information in the transcript may be interesting but may not relate to your question.

3. Eliminate all highlighted data that are not related to your question; however, start a separate file to store unrelated data. You may want to come back and reevaluate these data in the future.

4. Take each item of data and code or give a descriptor for the data. The descriptor or name will often be a characteristic word from within the data.

5. Cluster the items of data that are related or connected in some way and begin to develop patterns.

6. Patterns that are related to a preexisting theme are placed together with any other patterns that correspond with the theme, along with direct quotes taken from the data (transcribed interviews, field notes, documents, etc.) to elucidate the pattern.

7. Any patterns that do not relate to preexisting themes should be kept in a separate file for future evaluation of the meanings as they relate to the overall topic.

Repeat Steps 1–7 for each participant's data

8. Now revisit the patterns that did not fit the preexisting categories and remain open to any new patterns and themes that are related to the research topic and have emerged from the data analysis.

9. Each pattern should be described and elucidated by supporting quotes from the data.

10. For each theme, the researcher needs to write a detailed analysis describing the scope and substance of each theme.

11. Finally, the data are synthesized together to form a composite synthesis of the question under inquiry.

Thematic analysis with CC

Thematic analysis with CC can be either IA or ThA. The difference is that the data collected are analyzed as they are collected. The analysis begins during the collection of data. The first participant's data are analyzed, and as each subsequent participant's data are analyzed, they are compared to the previously analyzed data and combined with already developed patterns. The analysis constantly moves back and forth between current data and the data that have already been coded and clustered into patterns. Patterns and themes will change and grow throughout the process as the analysis continues.

Step-by-step analysis

1. Review and familiarize yourself with the data collected from the first participant (interviews, journals, field notes, records, documents, etc.). Read the documents and highlight intuitively any sentences, phrases, or paragraphs that appear to be meaningful.

2. Review the highlighted data, and use your research question to decide if the highlighted data are related to your question. Some information in the transcript may be interesting, but not relate to your question.

3. Eliminate all highlighted data that are not related to your question; however, start a separate file to store unrelated data. You may want to come back and reevaluate these data in the future.

4. Data that are determined to be relevant to the research question are called meaning units. Meaning units consist of direct quotes from the transcribed interviews (or other narrative data). Create a code for each meaning unit.

5. Cluster the meaning units that are related or connected in some way and begin to develop patterns.

6. Complete this process for the first participant's data. The researcher codes and clusters the first participant's data and, as each subsequent participant's data are analyzed, they are compared to the previously analyzed data. Throughout this process, each participant's data are reviewed and analyzed, and the researcher is comparing, contrasting, and combining the data being analyzed with the data that were previously analyzed. Thus, it is a CC procedure.

7. Throughout this process, data that correspond to a specific pattern are identified and placed with the corresponding pattern and direct quotes are taken from the data (transcribed interviews, field notes, documents, etc.) to elucidate the pattern.

8. Throughout the process, take all the patterns and look for the emergence of overarching themes. This process involves

combining and clustering the related patterns into themes. "A theme captures something important about the data in relation to the research question and represents some level of patterned response of meaning within the data set" (Braun & Clarke, 2006, p. 80).

9. Patterns and themes may tend to shift and change throughout the process of analysis.
10. After all the data have been analyzed, arrange the themes to correspond with the supporting patterns. The patterns are used to elucidate the themes.
11. For each theme, the researcher writes a detailed analysis describing the scope and substance of each theme.
12. Each pattern should be described and elucidated by supporting quotes from the data.
13. The data are synthesized together to form a composite synthesis of the data answering the question under inquiry.

The step-by-step presentation of the three types of thematic analysis has been adapted and modified from Percy et al. (2015).

Note: In all three of the versions of the thematic analysis, be sure that your direct quotes from the data that are used in developing your narrative or used to exemplify a pattern or theme are long enough to convey meaning. Read the selected quotes; is there enough information to convey meaning? If not, add more to the quote by using a larger portion of the data. The quote must make sense to the reader.

Member checking

Member checking occurs when data collection and data analysis are completed. Whether or not you use member checking is dependent on the topic and the feasibility of being able to contact participants after the interviews. If you use member checking, it should be explained in your research plan.

Creswell (2007) suggested member checking as a way of verifying that you have accurately captured the experiences of your participants. "This approach, *writ large* in most qualitative studies, involves taking data, analyses, interpretations, and conclusions back to the participants so that they can judge the accuracy and credibility of the account" (p. 208).

Member checking can be used for validation of your findings (Moustakas, 1994, pp. 110–111). The process for using member checking might be a follow-up phone interview with a time range of 15–30 minutes. For the thematic IA and ThA procedures, the member checking could occur after the themes for each participant have been developed. For the thematic analysis with CC the member checking needs to happen after the composite synthesis is drafted because patterns and themes are a composite of the data developed from all the participants.

During the member checking process, the researcher shares their findings and asks for feedback from the participant. The participant may verify the findings or discuss any discrepancies. If there were any differences, the researcher considers the discrepancies and makes revisions as needed.

After the findings have been discussed, the researcher asks the participant if they would like to add any additional information they thought about since their involvement in the study. This is an opportunity to gather more data to your investigation. The new information would be discussed during the follow-up interview and then added to the data analysis. Member checking can be a valuable aspect of validity.

There is controversy regarding the use and meaning of the term validity in qualitative research. According to Winter, (2000), "The exact nature of 'validity' is a highly debated topic in both educational and social research since there exists no single or common definition of the term" (p. 1). However, it was repeatedly noted that an important aspect of validity in qualitative research is being able to justify the findings (Winter, 2000).

When using generic qualitative research to conduct a dissertation, the researcher demonstrates validity by the extent in which the study represents the phenomenon that it was intended to describe. The researcher is concerned with evaluations of the data collection procedures, the research design, the data analysis methods, and the presentation of the findings of the study. Validity is based on the assessment of whether the findings accurately describe the phenomena under inquiry. In addition, validity addresses the skills of the researcher that has conducted the study. Therefore, the researcher stays aware of validity throughout each step of the dissertation research process.

Data storage and management

Research data collected and data analyzed using any of the three types of thematic analysis must be stored in a manner that is protected from loss and insures participant confidentiality. Research data include printed and electronic versions of communication with participants, field notes, journal documents, narrative descriptions, as well as audio-recorded interviews and analyzed data. Whether these data are in printed form or electronic form (computer files stored on the computer or on thumb drives, CDs, external hard drives) it should be stored in a safe deposit box or a fireproof and waterproof safe or file cabinet. These means of storage must be locked, and the only person with access should be the researcher. Additionally, the researcher's phone and computer must be password protected. If data are being transported it must be done so in a locked valise.

Data should be stored on computer files and managed using either word processing programs such as MS Word or Google Docs, or a software program designed to work with qualitative research studies such as Dedoose, MAXODA, NVivo, and ATLAS.ti.

Note that while these qualitative research software programs provide an excellent way to store and manage data, especially for computer savvy researchers, they do not analyze the data. "But the computers don't do the thinking needed to move a study along. Only a person can do that" (Corbin & Strauss, 2008, p. 201).

Chapter 7, the presentation of the data, will discuss information that needs to be briefly repeated from your research plan or proposal. It offers suggestions for how to present the description of the sample. There will be guidelines for how to ideally describe and present your data analysis process and create your composite synthesis.

Presentation of the data

This chapter provides a detailed description of how the researcher presents the data after the data were collected and analyzed for a generic qualitative dissertation. Setting the stage for the data presentation begins with a restatement of and discussion about the research question, and a description of the sample. The researcher restates the research question providing a brief synopsis of the significance of the topic and the researcher's relationship with the topic under investigation. The data presentation is organized to provide a detailed step-by-step demonstration of the analysis process for the purpose of providing a clear depiction of how the data were analyzed and interpreted. A clear presentation of the data allows the reader to evaluate the trustworthiness of the study.

Sample

Describing the sample begins with the sample size. The demographic description of the sample presents information about the people who participated in the study. Commonly used

DOI: 10.4324/9781003195689-7

demographic information includes participant age, gender, ethnicity, educational status, and area of residence; however, the demographics vary depending on the research topic and the research question. The demographics presented must have relevance to the research question. If your topic was the experience of divorce for people with a membership in an organized religion, the demographics might include religion, number of years married, and the number of children. Educational status and area of residence would not be essential demographics for this topic.

When describing the sample be certain to protect the identity of the participants and to maintain their confidentiality so that a reader of the dissertation manuscript is unable to determine the identity of individual participants in the study. If the researcher describes participants individually in a detailed narrative style, there is a potential risk of breaching confidentiality.

There are two suggestions for addressing confidentiality when describing the demographics of the participants. One way is to describe the sample as a whole. For example, suppose the topic is on the experience of helping professionals living in a small rural area. The demographics could be presented in the following manner:

> The sample consisted of 10 participants who ranged from 35–50 years of age. There were five males and five females; five were African American, four were Caucasian, one Hispanic. All participants had college degrees in the social sciences, with an average of 11 years practicing in a small rural area of the United States.

Another method for describing the sample is by using Table 7.1.

Table 7.1
Example of presentation of sample characteristics

Participant no.	Gender	Ethnicity	Age	College degree	No. of years practicing in rural area
P1	F	African American	37	MSW	10
P2	M	Caucasian	50	MSN	18
P3	F	Hispanic	35	MA	8

Presentation of the data

Introduce your generic qualitative study data with a statement about the type of thematic analysis applied to your data collected from the participants. The data analysis process for a generic qualitative study must be presented in the dissertation manuscript and must be presented in a manner consistent with the type of thematic analysis used to analyze the data.

The guidelines for the presentation of the data are described separately for the three types of thematic analysis: inductive analysis, theoretical analysis, and thematic analysis with constant comparison.

Inductive analysis

Inductive analysis is data driven, and there was no attempt to fit the data into any preexisting categories. The researcher set aside all pre-understandings and preconceived ideas. The data collected from each participant were analyzed individually. During this process, the researcher immersed themselves in each individual participant's data.

The aspects of the data analysis process are interpreted and explained by the researcher throughout the data presentation. The researcher describes how the data were analyzed individually. The researcher illustrates how the patterns emerged from the data and how patterns were clustered to construct the themes.

Step-by-step analysis presentation of data

1. The researcher reviewed and read all the data collected from the first participant. The researcher read the documents and highlighted intuitively any sentences, phrases, or paragraphs that appeared to be meaningful.

2. The researcher reviewed the highlighted data and used the research question to decide if the highlighted data were related to answering the research question. Some information in the transcript may have been interesting but did not relate to the research question.

3. The researcher set aside all highlighted data that were not related to the research question. The researcher started a separate file to store this data. The researcher saved this folder in order to reevaluate the data at a future time.

4. The data that were determined to be relevant to the research question were called meaning units. Meaning units were direct quotes from the data collected. A code was created for each meaning unit.

5. The researcher clustered the meaning units that were related or connected in some manner and began the process of developing patterns. The initial codes were written in pencil in order to rename codes during the process of developing patterns. The coding evolved as the researcher sought meanings and explanations by asking, "What is happening here?" This process led to determining names for each identified pattern.

6. After the researcher listed the meaning units under the corresponding pattern, the researcher read the quotes under each pattern to make sure the meaning units fit

under the pattern, and that the names of the patterns made sense.

7. The researcher wrote a brief description of the relationship of the pattern to answering the research question. Each pattern was interpreted and elucidated by supporting quotes from the data.

The presentation of the patterns and the supporting meaning units (direct quotes from the transcript) illustrates how the researcher developed patterns from the data. Table 7.2 presents a brief description of the patterns with examples of meaning units consisting of direct quotes from the participant's data, and the actual number of meaning units from data analyzed from participant 1.

Table 7.2
Participant 1 patterns

Patterns	Meaning units/ direct quotes	# Meaning units
Pattern 1 (1–3 sentences describing the relationship of the pattern to answering the research question)	Direct quote Direct quote Direct quote Direct quote Direct quote	8
Pattern 2	Direct quote Direct quote Direct quote Direct quote Direct quote	5
Pattern 3, etc.	Direct quote Direct quote Direct quote Direct quote Direct quote, etc.	6

Note. The number of meaning units presented will be dependent on the amount of data collected from each participant. To avoid redundancy or too many lengthy quotes, the researcher may decide to limit the quotes and choose not to present all the meaning units. The third column is for the actual number of meaning units.

The researcher took all the patterns from the first participant's data and looked for the emergence of overarching themes. This process involved combining and clustering the related patterns to create themes. "A theme captures something important about the data in relation to the research question and represents some level of patterned response of meaning within the data set" (Braun & Clarke, 2006, p. 80).

8. After all the data have been analyzed, the researcher arranged the themes to correspond with the supporting patterns. The patterns were listed under the theme. The patterns were used to elucidate the themes (Table 7.3).

For each theme, the researcher wrote a detailed analysis describing the scope and substance of each theme. Throughout the construction of the theme description, the

Table 7.3
Participant 1 themes

Themes	Patterns
Theme 1	Pattern 1 Pattern 2 Pattern 3, etc.
Theme 2	Pattern 1 Pattern 2 Pattern 3, etc.
Theme 3, etc.	Pattern 1 Pattern 2 Pattern 3, etc.

researcher may use direct quotes from the data to exemplify the theme description.

9. The researcher repeated this process for each participant's data.
10. Once the analysis was completed for all the participants, the repeating patterns and themes from all participants were brought together into a composite synthesis, which interprets the meanings and implications regarding the question under investigation.

Synthesis

When creating the composite synthesis for the generic qualitative dissertation the researcher seeks to bring together the meanings portrayed by the participants. The composite synthesis can take many creative forms. The researcher may develop a narrative that addresses the research question with an emphasis on giving the participants a voice. The synthesis could be a story or a poem. It may take the form of a process that describes the path from beginning to end.

Theoretical analysis

Theoretical analysis is employed in a situation in which the research topic has some predetermined categories (themes) to examine during the data analysis. The predetermined categories were stated in the research question. The researcher used their pre-understandings when conducting the data analysis. The researcher also remained open to the possibilities of new themes emerging from the thematic analysis process.

The aspects of the data analysis process are interpreted and explained by the researcher throughout the data presentation. The researcher describes how the data were analyzed individually. The researcher illustrates how the patterns emerged from the data and were organized under the appropriate preexisting themes, and how patterns that did not fit under preexisting themes were clustered together to create newly discovered themes that provide a deeper understanding of the phenomenon under investigation.

Step-by-step analysis presentation of data

1. The researcher read, reviewed, and became familiar with the data collected from each participant. The researcher re-read the data and highlighted intuitively any sentences, phrases, or paragraphs that appear to be meaningful. The researcher kept in mind the predetermined categories (themes) that were related to the topic under inquiry and was cognizant of remaining open to any new patterns and themes that related to the research question.

2. During this process, the researcher immersed themselves in each participant's data individually. The researcher reviewed the highlighted data and used the research question to decide if the highlighted data were related to the research question.

3. The researcher eliminated all highlighted data that were not related to the research question; however, started a separate file to store unrelated data for the purpose of future reevaluation.

4. The data that were determined to be relevant to the research question were called meaning units. Meaning units were direct quotes from the data collected. A code was created for each meaning unit.

5. The researcher clustered the meaning units that were related or connected in some way and developed patterns. The patterns were succinctly described, and the meaning units that supported each pattern were listed under the applicable pattern.

Participant 1 patterns

Pattern 1: Name of pattern and description

1. Meaning unit/direct quote.
2. Meaning unit/direct quote.
3. Meaning unit/direct quote, etc.

Pattern 2: Name of pattern and description

1. Meaning unit/direct quote.
2. Meaning unit/direct quote.
3. Meaning unit/direct quote, etc.

Etc.

6. Any patterns that did not correspond with preexisting themes were clustered together to formulate new discovered themes. The researcher presented the preexisting themes along with any newly discovered themes that emerged during the analysis for participant 1. Table 7.4 shows which patterns elucidate each theme.

    For each theme, the researcher developed a detailed analysis describing the scope and substance of each theme. Throughout the construction of the theme description, the researcher used direct quotes from the data to exemplify the theme description.

Table 7.4
Participant 1 themes

Themes	*Patterns*
Theme 1	Pattern 1 Pattern 2 Pattern 3, etc.
Theme 2	Pattern 1 Pattern 2 Pattern 3, etc.
Theme 3	Pattern 1 Pattern 2 Pattern 3, etc.
Theme 4 (newly discovered theme)	Pattern 1 Pattern 2 Patterns 3

7. The steps were repeated for all participants. The researcher approached each individual analysis with *fresh eyes* for the purpose of staying aware of individual differences and new discoveries.

8. The data from all the participants were synthesized together to form a composite synthesis of the question under inquiry.

Thematic analysis with constant comparison

Thematic analysis with constant comparison can be either inductive analysis or theoretical analysis. The constant comparison procedure is different because the analysis occurs throughout the data collection process. The data are analyzed as they are collected. The first participant's data are analyzed and, and as each subsequent participant's data are analyzed, they are compared and combined to the previously analyzed data. The analysis constantly moves back and forth between current data and the data that have already been coded and clustered into patterns. Patterns and themes will grow and evolve throughout the analysis process.

Step-by-step analysis presentation of data

1. The researcher reviewed and became familiar with the data collected from the first participant. The researcher read the documents and highlighted intuitively any sentences, phrases, or paragraphs that appeared to be meaningful.

2. The researcher reviewed the highlighted data and used the research question to decide if the highlighted data were related to the research question.

3. The researcher eliminated all highlighted data that were not related to the research question; the researcher started a separate file to store unrelated data in order to reevaluate this data in the future.

4. The data that were determined to be relevant to the research question were called meaning units. Meaning units were

direct quotes from the data collected. A code was created for each meaning unit.

5. The researcher clustered the meaning units that were related or connected in some manner and began the process of developing patterns.

6. After the researcher completed this process of developing the patterns for the first participant's data, the researcher continued the process of coding and clustering the meaning units with each subsequent participant's data. Throughout this process, as each participant's data were reviewed and analyzed, the researcher constantly compared the new data being analyzed with the data that had been previously analyzed. Thus, the patterns developed for participant 2 are compared and combined with participant 1. The patterns developed for participant 3 are compared with the combined patterns from participant 1 and participant 2.

7. Throughout this repeating process, meaning units that corresponded to a specific pattern were identified and placed with the corresponding pattern. Any meaning units that did not fit under an established pattern were set aside to assess if it were possible to develop a new pattern.

The presentation of the patterns and the supporting meaning units (direct quotes from the transcript) illustrates how the researcher interpreted patterns from the data. Table 7.5 includes a brief description of the patterns and examples of meaning units, and the actual number of meaning units from the data analyzed and combined for all participants.

Note. Because of the large number of patterns and direct quotes developed from combining the data for all participants, the researcher needs to limit the direct quotes. The number of quotations used will be dependent on the length of the quotes. The researcher needs to present enough quotes to support the pattern and to provide an understanding of how the patterns address answering the

Table 7.5
Patterns for all participants

Patterns	Meaning units/ direct quotes	# Of meaning units
Pattern 1 (for each pattern write one paragraph describing the relationship of the pattern toward answering the research question)	Direct quote (P6) Direct quote (P1) Direct quote (P3) Direct quote (P8) Direct quote (P7)	37
Pattern 2	Direct quote (P5) Direct quote (P1) Direct quote (P3) Direct quote (P4) Direct quote (P2)	47
Pattern 3	Direct quote (P1) Direct quote (P8) Direct quote (P5) Direct quote (P2) Direct quote (P7)	65
Pattern 4	Direct quote (P7) Direct quote (P1) Direct quote (P3) Direct quote (P5) Direct quote (P2)	88
Etc.		

research question. The researcher selects meaning units that are relevant examples so the reader can see the interrelationship between the meaning units, the patterns, and the research question. When choosing which meaning units to use for the presentation, it is important to make sure that all participants have a voice in this process. For some dissertations demonstrating that each participant in the study was included in the presentation of patterns can enhance credibility. This could be accomplished by indicating the participant number (P1, P2, etc.) for each direct quote.

8. Throughout the process, the researcher examined all patterns for the emergence of overarching themes. This process involved combining and clustering the related patterns into themes.

9. Patterns and themes were allowed to shift and evolve throughout the process of searching for the meanings of the phenomenon under inquiry. For the development of themes, the researcher thought about the underlying "how" of the experience, constantly questioning the data, with the desire of capturing the essence of the experience. Under what circumstances does the experience happen? What is the meaning? Are there any alternative meanings? etc.

10. After all the data had been analyzed and interpreted, the themes were arranged along with the patterns that were used to elucidate each theme.

   The researcher presents this data for the reader in a list of each theme with the corresponding patterns that support each theme.

   Note. A pattern can only support one theme.

   Theme 1
   1.1 Pattern
   1.2 Pattern
   1.3 Pattern
      etc.
   Theme 2
   2.1 Pattern
   2.2 Pattern
   2.3 Pattern
   2.4 Pattern
      etc.

11. The researcher set aside the analysis and returned with fresh eyes to re-read the data prior to creating the analytic description for each theme.

12. For each theme, the researcher wrote a detailed analysis describing the scope and substance of each theme. Throughout the construction of the theme description, the researcher used direct quotes from the data to exemplify the theme description.

Presentation of the theme analysis from the combined data from all participants

> Theme 1
>> (Theme Description)
> Theme 2
>> (Theme Description)
> Theme 3, Etc.
>> (Theme Description)
>> Etc.

13. The data were synthesized together to form a composite synthesis of the question under inquiry.

Note. When creating the composite synthesis for the generic qualitative dissertation the researcher seeks to bring together the meanings portrayed by the participants. The composite synthesis can take various creative forms. The researcher may develop a narrative that addresses the research question with an emphasis on giving their participants a voice. The synthesis could be a story or a poem. It may take the form of a process that describes the path taken to answer your research question.

Conclusion

This chapter consisted of suggestions about how to present your data analysis process and findings. By presenting an illustration of the step-by-step process it allows the reader to understand

how the findings were obtained and permits the reader to evaluate your analytic interpretations. The goal of the researcher
when presenting the data is to develop the presentation of the
data, in such a manner, that the readers is confident in the trustworthiness of the findings.

In Chapter 8, we offer information on how to summarize
the process of your completed dissertation journey. Important aspects of completing your dissertation are expanding the
meanings of your interpretations through the process of comparing your findings with the existing literature on the topic,
and your interpretations of the meanings inherent in results of
your research. The summary also illuminates the implications
and applications based on the results and explains the relevance
of the findings related to specific concerns in the social sciences.

Completing the journey

In this chapter we offer guidelines for completing your research journey. Throughout your dissertation process, you have enhanced your intuitions, creativity, and have matured academically. You have devoted your time and energy seeking understanding and meaning by listening, questioning, and investigating your participants' experiences. The data collection and data analysis were described through the lens of your participants' descriptions of their experience. In this chapter, your challenge is to make sense out of all you have digested during this process. In this final chapter of your dissertation, the researcher will reflect on the dissertation as a whole and use their insights and analytic skills to discuss and explain the meanings that have emerged during this journey.

The following sections offer suggestions for outlining the last chapter of the dissertation for a generic qualitative study. This final chapter may differ depending on the guidelines determined by your education institution. Students should consult with their educational institution and their doctoral committee for any specific structure stipulated for this final chapter of the dissertation.

DOI: 10.4324/9781003195689-8

Summary of the study

The summary of the study provides a logical progression of the overview of the study. A common way to begin the summary is to make a statement naming the research approach, the title of the study, and the research question. For example, a generic qualitative approach was used to conduct a study on the topic of...., followed by the research question that was used to guide each step of the dissertation.

Purpose

The summary describes the purpose of the study. When addressing the purpose of the study, think about the reasons for choosing your topic. What attracted you to this topic? What is the significance of this topic? What did you really want to know? What did you hope to accomplish by conducting this study?

Participants involved in the study

Summarize information about the participant's involvement. For example, 12 persons participated in the study. They all met the inclusion criteria of.... Their involvement in the study consisted of individual interviews and a follow-up interview that included member checking.

Methods

This section offers a brief overview of the methodology used in the study. What methods were used to collect, analyze, and present data?

The researcher's self-reflections

In the qualitative dissertation, it is common to offer critical self-reflections about the researcher's experiences during the dissertation process. Think about what stood out for you during your dissertation journey? What did you perceive as milestones during the process of the research? How did you experience the interview sessions? The researcher's critical self-reflections add to the reader's comprehension of how the dissertation process evolved and how the process was experienced. In each of the above sections the researcher may add personal thoughts on the dissertation process. The researcher might comment on the importance of the research question accurately addressing what the researcher was seeking to understand, or the research methods and procedures that enhanced or limited the investigation.

Results of the study

The researcher writes a narrative summary of the findings of the completed analysis that was presented in Chapter 7. In the generic qualitative dissertation, the patterns, themes, and synthesis are the findings.

Discussion of the results

At the end of Chapter 7, the researcher presented the findings that were developed from the patterns, themes, and synthesis specific to the participants' descriptions. Patton (2015) indicates that the process of making sense out of qualitative data is challenging and requires trust in the value of *inductive* theorizing.

> Design flexibility stems from the open-ended nature of naturalistic inquiry as well as pragmatic considerations. Being open and pragmatic requires a high tolerance for ambiguity and uncertainty as well as the trust in the ultimate value of what inductive analysis will yield.
>
> (p. 50)

The discussion in this section should pull together how the data were interpreted and the connection between the interpretations and the conception of meanings. Stake (2010) pointed out

that making sense of the data is about interpretation and determining what is meaningful. "Interpretation is an act of com-
position.... The best interpretations will be logical extensions
of the simple description but also will include contemplative,
speculative, even aesthetic extension" (p. 55). Central to this
process is demonstrating the conceptual relationships between
data, patterns, and themes.

Comparison to the literature

> Now that your investigation has been completed. How, in
> fact do your findings differ from findings presented in your
> literature review?
>
> (Moustakas, 1994, p. 184)

Prior to and while conducting your study you have reviewed
the literature published on your chosen topic. An aspect of discussing your results requires going back to the literature and
comparing the findings of your analysis with the literature published on your topic. The conceptions of meanings necessitate
comparing the findings, thus far, to relevant literature.

One way to approach this process is by comparing and contrasting the description of each developed theme from the analysis with the literature published on the subject. The researcher
interprets how the findings were similar and how they differed,
and illuminates on the meanings of new discoveries. This process is repeated with each theme developed during the data
analysis.

An additional suggestion is to "summarize core findings relevant to your research, differentiate your investigations from
prior research" (Moustakas, 1994, p. 183). This approach also
provides a platform for the researcher to review the existing literature on the topic and examine the findings of the researcher's
study to determine if the findings support the previous studies
and/or if the findings provide new information on the topic.

The researcher questions, did the results of this study add a deeper understanding of the topic under inquiry? If so, they elaborate on the significance of the new discoveries and deeper understandings. A critique of the results moves the presentation of the data to the next level.

Limitations of the study

All studies have limitations, whether they are quantitative, qualitative, or mixed methodology studies. For a qualitative study, the researcher evaluates the limitations of the study by critically examining the methodology and the conclusions based on the analysis.

For example, one limitation frequently cited in qualitative studies is that of the sampling strategy. Purposeful sampling strategy is commonly used in a generic qualitative dissertation. In using purposeful sampling, the researcher seeks information-rich cases and recruits participants with specific characteristics that will enable them to answer the research question. Because the selection of participants was based on the judgment and inclusion criteria determined by the researcher, it raises issues regarding researcher bias.

Another example of a possible limitation is that of the sample size in a qualitative study is small compared to a quantitative study. Although generalization is not a goal in the generic qualitative approach, a small sample size may be considered a limitation because the findings of the study do not lend itself to generalization.

The summary of the study addresses any problems you might have encountered: for example, difficulties with recruiting enough participants. Or a problem with an interview in which the participant was unable to verbalize their experience, resulting in insufficient data. As a result of a careful assessment of the limitations, the researcher should explain each design flaw or problem and how the issue(s) were resolved.

Implications and application of the study

> What implications, if any, are relevant to society? To your profession? To education? To you as a learner and as a person?
>
> (Moustakas, 1994, p. 184)

This section addresses the application and implications of the information discovered through the qualitative investigation. The researcher explores how the results of the study are relevant and how they can be applied to the field of study.

The concluding questions to be answered in this section ask who benefits from this study, what the implications of your research findings mean towards future visions, and how the implications of your research findings can be used to facilitate new directions.

The questions you need to answer regarding the applications of your study are based on the literature review of your topic during the dissertation process, the results of your study, and your increased knowledge about your topic. It is helpful to review the sections in your dissertation on the problem statement, the discussion of the findings, and the limitations of the study. Think about any questions that have arisen from your study. Consider what future studies on your topic would be advantageous for a specific population or for a particular social problem. The central question to answer is, what future research will bring forth relevance and meaning?

Conclusions

We believe that the generic qualitative research approach can be a trustworthy choice for a dissertation in the social sciences. However, this choice should only be made after a careful exploration of the research topic and a commitment to conduct a purposeful and rigorous dissertation.

During our years of serving on dissertation committees, we have experienced dedicated students struggling with understanding both the nuances and the procedures of qualitative research. This book was written with these students in mind. It was not meant to be a textbook, or the be-all-end-all for learning about qualitative research. This book was written for students who are seeking direction for how to use a generic qualitative approach to conduct a meaningful dissertation that is rigorous, credible, and trustworthy.

Considering the growth of the generic qualitative dissertations in the field of social sciences, it is our hope that we have been able to offer valuable information not only about how to organize and conduct a trustworthy generic qualitative dissertation but also about how to appreciate and enjoy the dissertation journey. Our hopes are that years after you have completed your dissertation, you will look back at your dissertation with pride in your accomplishments, and that your dissertation journey will always bring back fond memories.

References

Aronson, J. (1994). *A Pragmatic View of Thematic Analysis*. The Qualitative Report, 2, Number 1. Retrieved January 20, 2003, from http://www.nova.edu/ssss/QR/index.html

Bandura, A. (2006). Toward a psychology of human agency. *Perspectives on Psychological Science*, 1(2), 164–180. doi:10.1111/j.1745–6916.2006.00011.x

Berg, B.L. & Lune, H. (2012). *Qualitative research methods for the social sciences.* (8th ed). Upper Saddle River, NJ: Pearson.

Berger, P.L. & Luckmann, T. (1966). *The social construction of reality.* Garden City, NY: Doubleday.

Boateng, W. (2012). Evaluating the efficacy of Focus Group Discussion (FGD) in qualitative social research. *International Journal of Business and Social Science*, 3, 156–175.

Bogdan, R. & Taylor, S. (1975). *Introduction to qualitative research methods.* New York: John Wiley & Sons, Inc.

Bowen, A.G. (2008). Naturalistic inquiry and the saturation concept: A research note. *Qualitative Research*, 8(1), 137–152.

Braun, V. & Clarke, V. (2006). Using thematic analysis in psychology. *Qualitative Research in Psychology*, 3, 77–101. doi:10.1191/1478088706qp063oa

Caelli, K., Ray, L., & Mill, J. (2003). 'Clear as mud': Toward greater clarity in generic qualitative research. *International Journal of Qualitative Methods*, 2(2), 1–27.

Camic, P.M., Rhodes, J.E., & Yardley, L. (Eds.). (2003). *Qualitative research in psychology: Expanding perspectives in methodology and design*. Washington, DC: American Psychological Association.

Charmaz, K. (2006). *Constructing grounded theory: A practical guide through qualitative analysis*. London: Sage Publications, Inc.

Charmaz, K. (2014). *Constructing grounded theory*. (2nd ed). London: Sage publications, Inc.

Cooper, S. & Endacott, R. (2007). Generic qualitative research: A design for qualitative research in emergency care? *Emergency Medicine Journal: EMJ*, 24(12), 816–819.

Corbin, J. & Strauss, A. (2008). *Basics of qualitative research*. (3rd ed). Thousand Oaks, CA: Sage Publication, Inc.

Creswell, J. (1998). *Qualitative inquiry and research design: Choosing among five traditions*. Thousand Oaks, CA: Sage Publications, Inc.

Creswell, J. (2007). *Qualitative inquiry and research design: Choosing among five traditions*. (2nd ed). Thousand Oaks, CA: Sage Publications, Inc.

Creswell, J. (2018). *Qualitative inquiry and research design: Choosing among five traditions*. (4th ed). Thousand Oaks, CA: Sage Publications, Inc.

Dahlberg, K., Drew, N., & Nystrom, M. (2002). *Reflective life-world research*. Lund: Studentlitteratur AB.

Gadamer, H.G. (1975). *Truth and method*. New York: Seabury.

Golden, J., Piedmont, R.L., Ciarrocchi, J.W., & Rodgerson, T. (2004). Spirituality and burnout: An incremental validity study. *Journal of Psychology and Theology*, 32(2), 115–125. doi:10.1177/009164710403200204

Janis, I.L. (1972). *Victims of groupthink: A psychological study of foreign-policy decisions and fiascoes*. Boston, MA: Houghton Mifflin.

Janis, I.L. & Janis, I.L. (1982). *Groupthink: Psychological studies of policy decisions and fiascoes* (Vol. 349). Boston, MA: Houghton Mifflin.

Kennedy, D.M. (2016). Is it any clearer? Generic qualitative inquiry and the VSAUEEDC Model of DATA Analysis. *The Qualitative Report*, 21(8), 1369–1379. Retrieved from http://nsuworks.nova.edu/tqr/vol21/iss8/1

Merriam, S.B. (1998). *Qualitative research and case study applications in education*. San Francisco, CA: Jossey-Bass.

Merriam, S.B. (2009). *Qualitative research: A guide to design and implementations*. (3rd ed). San Francisco, CA: Jossey-Bass.

Morse, J. & Richards, L. (2002). *Read first for a user's guide to qualitative methods*. Thousand Oaks, CA: Sage Publications, Inc.

Moustakas, C. (1994). *Phenomenological research*. Thousand Oaks, CA: Sage Publications, Inc.

Patton, M.Q. (1990). *Qualitative evaluation and research methods*. (2nd ed). Thousand Oaks, CA: Sage Publications, Inc.

Patton, M.Q. (2002). *Qualitative research and evaluation methods*. (3rd ed). Thousand Oaks, CA: Sage Publications, Inc.

Patton, M.Q. (2015). *Qualitative research and evaluation methods*. (4th ed). Thousand Oaks, CA: Sage Publications, Inc.

Percy, W., Kostere, K., & Kostere, S. (2008). Generic qualitative research in psychology. Unpublished manuscript. Department of Psychology, Capella University.

Percy, W., Kostere, K., & Kostere, S. (2015). Generic qualitative research in psychology. *The Qualitative Report*, 20(2), 76–85. Retrieved from http://nsuworks.nova.edu/tqr/vol20/iss2/7/

Polkinghorne, D.E. (2005). Language and meaning: Data collection in qualitative research. *Journal of Counseling Psychology*, 52(2), 137–145.

Progoff, I. (1975). *At a journal workshop: The basic text and guide for using the Intensive Journal*. New York: Dialogue House Library.

de Saint-Exupery, A. (1943). *The little prince*. San Diego: CA: Harcourt, Inc.

Stake, R. (1995). *The art of case study research*. Thousand Oaks, CA: Sage Publications, Inc.

Stake, R. (2010). *Qualitative research: Studying how things work*. New York: The Guilford Press.

Tashakkori, A. & Teddlie, C. (1998). *Mixed methodology: Combining qualitative and quantitative approaches*. Thousand Oaks, CA: Sage Publications, Inc.

Taylor, S. & Bogdan, R. (1998). *Introduction to qualitative research methods*. (3rd ed). New York: Wiley & Sons, Inc.

Winter, G. (2000). A comparative discussion of the notion of 'validity' in qualitative and quantitative research. *The Qualitative Report*, 4(3/4). Retrieved from http://www.nova.edu/ssss/QR/QR4-3/winter.html

Index

For Product Safety Concerns and Information please contact our EU
representative GPSR@taylorandfrancis.com
Taylor & Francis Verlag GmbH, Kaufingerstraße 24, 80331 München, Germany

www.ingramcontent.com/pod-product-compliance
Lightning Source LLC
Chambersburg PA
CBHW071104280326
41928CB00052B/2858